ENDORSEMENTS

For many of us, we often think too little of our work or swing to the other extreme and think too much of it. As always, God's Word strikes the perfect balance between the two and instructs us how to view our work as "unto the Lord." In her book, LIFE PURPOSE: The Joy of Doing What God Created You to Do, Joanne Hawes clearly draws from Scripture practical guidance for how we should approach our work and rest in God's calling for us.

Wayne Shepherd
Christian Radio Host

The truths in this book were originally taught by Joanne Hawes in the Life Purpose Workshop. I attended that workshop 18 years ago and it deeply impacted my life. Joanne's teaching helped me to recognize *who* I am in Jesus. It gave me an understanding of my God-given gift and guided me into my passions for my work. LIFE PURPOSE: The Joy of Doing What God Created You to Do is a must read for every believer.

Kathy Penfield
Licensed MFT

LIFE PURPOSE:

The Joy of Doing What God Created You to Do

LIFE PURPOSE:
The Joy of Doing What God Created You to Do

By Joanne Hawes

with

Janne L. Copley

LIFE PURPOSE
PUBLISHING LLC

Phoenix, Arizona
www.lifepurpose.com

All stories in this book are true. In some instances, names have been changed.

Edited by: Louise Damberg
Cover and interior design: Michelle Radomski at OneVoiceCan.com
Cover Photo: Getty Images stock: Joy

ISBN 978-0-9895665-0-6

Published by Life Purpose Publishing LLC
1334 E. Myrtle Avenue
Phoenix, AZ 85020
WWW.LIFEPURPOSE.COM

Printed in the United States of America

DEDICATION

This book is dedicated to Butch Hawes, the love of my life.

CONTENTS

FOREWORD

I met Joanne and Butch Hawes when I attended the Life Purpose Workshop almost seventeen years ago. Their passion to see God's people set free from the mundane to pursue their God-given purpose in their daily lives and work was inspirational. It was Joanne's teaching, now contained in this book, that eventually set both me and my husband free to experience the joy of knowing who God created us to be and to do what He designed us to do.

Joanne has been on a thirty-year journey of developing, living, and teaching God's truths about work. She has moved from climbing the corporate ladder to obeying God's directive to quit her job and help rebuild her husband's business. God birthed Life Purpose Ministries in her heart in 1990. Joanne began writing this book because people were clamoring for it. She finished writing this book because of God's revealed will.

LIFE PURPOSE: The Joy of Doing What God Created You to Do has been eight years in the writing. The penning of this book has been a journey. It has been a time where God has required that His truths, contained in this teaching, be lived before they were published. Joanne has done that. With God's help, she has broken free from the emptiness of the secular world system. She has traveled through the wilderness to discover the reality of serving God. She has learned the difficult, but true, lesson that her provision comes from Him. She is enjoying living and working in her God-appointed sphere of influence and authority.

As Joanne continues to pursue God's purpose for her daily life and work on earth, she is looking forward to continuing her journey in eternity.

1

It has been an honor and a privilege to be a God-ordained fellow traveler with Joanne in the writing of this book. My life will never be the same.

Janne L. Copley
Co-writer

INTRODUCTION

"Trust in the Lord with all your heart and do not lean on your own understanding. In all your ways acknowledge Him, and He will make your paths straight."
—-PROVERBS 3:5, 6 (NAS)

Joanne's Story

I prayed to receive Jesus Christ as my Savior in 1979. I was fortunate to have a coworker, Don, who along with his wife, Pat, shared the gospel of Jesus Christ with me and discipled me for three years. Don and Pat's teaching provided me with a solid, biblical foundation for learning God's truths. Don challenged me to commit my entire life to God and serve Him daily.

Given that challenge, I asked myself what it truly meant to serve God. What would it look and feel like if I served God on a daily basis? Did it mean that I should go to a new church, attend Bible College or become involved in some sort of ministry?

I decided the best source for discovering the answers to my questions would be to go directly to God. I asked Him to give me understanding and teach me what it meant to serve Him on a daily basis. The answer that came to me was that because my job was such a major part of my life I could study the Bible to learn God's perspective regarding work. I got down on my knees that same day and committed my vocation to God. I asked Him to reveal His truths to me and help me apply them to my everyday life.

At that time I worked in computer-aided design and development for a large corporation. Similar to many workers I was in the process of climbing the corporate ladder, driven to

3

make as much money as possible. I had gone through a divorce before accepting Jesus Christ as my Savior. Leary of relationships, I had made a decision to remain single; however, God had other plans. The Lord introduced me to my future husband, Ernest 'Butch' Hawes, at our local church group in 1987.

Butch and I were on a plane after a short courtship and engagement, headed to Indiana so he could meet my family. It was at that time he confessed to me his business was 'belly up' and he was heavily in debt. He was committed to paying all that he owed but could not see how it was humanly possible. We prayed right there on the plane for God's intervention, trusting He had a plan and purpose for our lives. We committed our marriage to God and asked Him to release us from the bondage of debt so we could freely serve Him. We married in September of 1987.

God began a process in my life a few months later that challenged my beliefs and stretched me beyond anything I could have imagined. During my daily prayer time, I sensed God was asking me to step out in faith and quit my job. "Quit my job?" I asked. My paycheck was our only source of income. Surely we needed it to pay our bills and 'put food on the table'. Having finally gained the status, position, and salary I had been striving toward, how could God be asking me to walk away from a twenty-year career? What would I do with the rest of my life?

The more I thought about what God was asking me to do and pondered the truths He had been teaching me, I recognized disobedience was not an option.

When I shared with Butch what God had put in my heart, we prayed about it for at least six months. We both wanted to obey

God but we also wanted to make sure He was, in fact, directing me to quit my job.

In August of 1989 we made the decision I would resign from my job at the end of the year. God revealed His timetable the same day we had made the decision when the company I was working for announced they were downsizing. They were asking volunteers to step forward immediately. Driving home that same day, God impressed on me that I should accept the modest severance package and begin working with Butch to rebuild his general contracting firm. Quitting my job and going to work with my husband was the first step of obedience that led to the birth of Life Purpose Ministries and the development of the Life Purpose Workshop. Ultimately, it also led to the writing of this book.

Putting myself into God's hands was by far one of the most rewarding, yet challenging, journeys of my Christian life. For me it was the pathway toward physical, financial, and spiritual freedom through my relationship with Jesus Christ. Learning to trust God one day at a time allowed Him to begin the process of realigning my steps to bring me into the fullness of His plans and purposes for my daily life and work. This process continues today.

Perhaps you can identify with my story. You have a desire to serve God but somewhere along the way you veered off course. You feel as though you are stuck in your present situation having missed the target of God's will in spite of your sincere efforts to serve Him. You have a need for a spiritual connection and a desire for fulfillment that continues to remain unmet.

LIFE PURPOSE: The Joy of Doing What God Created

You to Do will help you experience the fullness of God's plans and purposes for your daily life and work. The truths presented in this book will be the start of a lifelong journey that will dramatically alter your relationship with your Creator. Your understanding of God will shift from the mundane of the everyday to the expansiveness of the eternal. You will gain a deep sense of personal fulfillment, heartfelt peace, and the joy of knowing and experiencing *who* God created you to be and *what* He designed you to do. Let's begin with an understanding of what your life may look like today...

CHAPTER ONE

Between Two Worlds

From the Cage to the Kingdom

"For we are His workmanship, created in Christ Jesus for good works, which God prepared beforehand so that we would walk in them."
— EPHESIANS 2:10 (NAS)

I heard a story delivered by Dr. David Moore on his *Moore on Life* radio program a number of years ago about a large zoo that had been given the unexpected gift of a full-grown polar bear. The zoo was in the midst of a fund-raising campaign, and renovations were still being planned, so it would be easy for the architect to go back to the drawing board to design a new home for the bear. The new habitat would be done in a relatively short period of time, or so the zoo officials thought.

Progress was much slower than anticipated. What should have been a three- to four-month stay in temporary quarters for the bear stretched into more than a year. While this was not a matter of life or death, the bear's range of movement in his temporary cage was limited to three steps to the left and three to the right.

Finally, the new habitat was completed. Excitement ran high as the staff watched the bear's release into his new environment. The surroundings were so massive compared to the temporary cage that the bear appeared dwarfed. He stood in the center of his new home, head swaying from side to side. Slowly the bear lifted a paw and took a step to the right.   Then he took another and another. Suddenly, to the astonishment of those watching, the bear stopped. He then took exactly three steps to the left. The anticipation, previously so high among the crowd, vanished as the bear's movements were limited to the smallness of his former temporary cage. It took several weeks for him to break free from the limitations of his past.

By designing a home as similar as possible to his natural habitat, the zoo had done its best to enable the bear to live a bear's life. Unfortunately, the bear was operating in a different reality. His old cage exerted more influence over him than his new environment so, initially, he was unable to enjoy the vastness of his new surroundings. The bear's reality was the cage.

This same truth can be applied to the lives of God's people. God has prepared a place for each of us, but our past experiences prevent us from enjoying the benefits of our salvation. Our experience exerts more influence than the freedom God has prepared for us. Fearful of change, we prefer to hang onto the perceived security of 'cage life'.

Perhaps cage life is your reality. When God led me to leave the corporate world, it took me almost a year to do so because corporate life was familiar to me. God was asking me to trust Him to free me from the false beliefs that prevented me from experiencing all that He had prepared for me. Only after making the decision to follow God's leading to leave my job was I able to begin to experience the fullness of the new life God had planned for me.

Janne's experience was similar to mine. She began to grasp the biblical concepts about work when she attended the Life Purpose Workshop in 1996. Just as the bear had difficulty expanding into his new environment, Janne was limited by her past. She longed to experience God's plans and purposes for her life but was reluctant to believe His promises were hers for the taking. She was weary of cage life but too frightened to move beyond her present circumstances.

Discovering God's truths about work was the start of a lifelong process for Janne. Today she is living and working in the mountains of Colorado, experiencing the joy and peace of serving God right where He placed her—in her home! The journey has not always been easy, but God has been faithful. He continues to reveal His plans and purposes for Janne and empower her to complete the work He has prepared for her.

How would you describe your reality today? Are you participating in the fullness of God's plans and purposes for your daily life and work? Or are you identifying with the bear? Do you find yourself taking three steps to the right and three to the left, going nowhere? Are you locked in your past experiences, too frightened to venture out and explore all God has created you to be and do? If cage life is your reality, you have probably already discovered it is seldom rewarding. It leaves you yearning for something more.

MANY PEOPLE ARE DISSATISFIED WITH THEIR WORK LIFE

If you feel dissatisfied with your daily work life, I assure you that you are not alone. A 2012 survey conducted by Right Management, part of the staffing firm Manpower Group, reveals that 81 % of all people are dissatisfied with their work life. Since work comprises such a large part of our lives, this statistic may also represent how we feel about life in general. Those who already have a personal relationship with Christ are included in this figure. This statistic has been substantiated in more than ten years of having taught the Life Purpose Workshop throughout the United States and Canada and conferring with thousands of people, personally and on radio.

When I asked people to choose a color to describe how they felt about their work life, 85 % selected colors that represented dissatisfaction. Many people chose red, indicating they felt as though they were in a fire with no means of escape. Others chose brown, signifying they felt as though they were stuck in the mud. Gray symbolized neutrality or a lack of excitement. The most common color was black, meaning the people felt limp or lifeless, without hope. Those who were working only for money chose green.

Why is it that a personal relationship with Jesus Christ makes no noticeable difference in the way we feel about our work? Were there more non-Christians than Christians included in the workshops, causing the statistics to be skewed? No. Approximately 99 % of all people who attended the Life Purpose Workshop over a ten-year period were Christians; yet, most experienced little or no relevance between God and work. As believers, they recognized a need to serve Christ in their workplace but were unable to bridge the gap between biblical truths and their workweek. It is no surprise that this limited their potential to serve God with joy and experience fulfillment.

"It has been estimated there are at least forty thousand different occupations in the United States. Yet, for all that, only a small percentage of the population is completely satisfied with their responsibilities. Personnel problems, the lack of adequate pay, and wearisome hours of routine tasks are only some of the reasons. Few people, if any, are truly satisfied," writes Erwin W. Lutzer in his book *One Minute after You Die*.

Perhaps you can identify with these feelings of dissatisfaction. Given an opportunity to choose a color that represents how you feel about your work, what color would it be? Would your color reveal that you feel frustrated, unfulfilled, or disillusioned? Would it show you feel driven to find purpose and meaning for your work life or that you are resting in God, trusting Him to reveal His plans for you?

When we choose work that is contrary to God's design for our lives, it creates feelings of restlessness, discontent, and depression. This affects every area of our lives—our relationship with God, our relationships with our family and friends, our emotional and physical well-being, and our health and motivation. As Jose Ortega Gasset wrote in *The Dehumanization of Art*, "Persistent depression is only too clearly the sign that a man is living contrary to his vocation."

If we live in ignorance of what God desires for our lives, it cripples us because it limits our understanding of *who* He has created us to be. We simply cannot see the glistening, unexplored vistas that surround us as children of God. Without the clarity of God's sight and teaching, we can only experience cage life.

WE ARE CREATED TO SERVE AND GLORIFY GOD

According to Biblegateway.com, the word *work* is mentioned 689 times in the Bible (KJV) which tells us God has many important things to say about it. Based on the number of times work is mentioned in God's Word, its importance is second only to salvation. This is a very bold statement and worth repeating: work is second only to your salvation. Why? Because God created us with a unique purpose. He prepared work in advance for us that is purposeful and rewarding. We have been created to serve and glorify God in a particular manner and in a

11

specific environment—in our homes, schools, neighborhoods, marketplace, churches, or religious organizations. When we are doing the work God prepared for us, in the place He has called us to serve, it is our full-time ministry.

If work is second only to salvation, we need to develop an understanding that biblical work is more than a job or a means to a paycheck. "Work is not primarily a thing one does to live but the thing one lives to do. It is, or should be, the full expression of the worker's faculties, the thing in which he finds spiritual, mental, and bodily satisfaction," states Dorothy L. Sayers in *Unpopular Opinions*.

"It is not only prayer that gives God glory but work. Smiting on an anvil, sawing a beam, whitewashing a wall, driving horses, sweeping, scouring, everything gives God glory if being in His grace you do it as your duty. To go to Communion worthily gives God great glory, but a man with a dung fork in his hand, a woman with a slop pail, give Him glory, too. He is so great that all things give Him glory if you mean they should," writes Gerard Manley Hopkins in *The Principle or Foundation*.

When we accept Jesus Christ as our Savior, the most important thing we can do is to love and serve Him in ways that are consistent with how He made us. If God created you to be a homemaker, be the best homemaker you can be, serving your family with gladness. If He designed you to teach, teach others as you would want to be taught. If you are called to work within the service industry, serve others as you would want to be served. When we function in ways that fit with God's design for us, we naturally fulfill His plans and purposes for our lives.

God has called each one of us to stand alongside the great men and women of faith who heeded His call in their lives. We are called to stand with Abraham, Isaac, Esther, Ruth, Moses, Joseph, Elizabeth, Paul, and Lydia, to name a few. He has designed us for service to the King of kings and Lord of lords, just as He designed them. Consider that God knew you while you were still in your mother's womb:

"For You formed my inward parts; You wove me in my mother's womb." —PSALM 139:13 (NAS)

God also prepared work in advance for us:

"For we are God's handiwork, created in Christ Jesus to do good works, which God prepared in advance for us to do."
—EPHESIANS 2:10

God designed you precisely according to His plans and purposes, and He wants you to experience all the benefits of your salvation.

GOD DESIGNED YOU FOR SUCCESS

As you learn and apply God's truths about work, you may find living a life centered in Christ looks upside down in the eyes of the world. Why? Because worldly success is directly opposite to God's view of success. In the world, we are pressured to achieve greatness. Success is measured by the size of our paycheck, our job title, the way we dress, and where we live. While there is nothing wrong with the niceties of life, God does not measure success or greatness by these standards. In John 17:4 Jesus, Himself, defined true success when He said to His Father:

"I have brought you glory on earth by finishing the work you gave me to do."

To experience and embrace biblical success, you must be in exactly the right position. The good news is that when you choose to make your life's journey in the context of a personal relationship with God through His Son, Jesus Christ, you are moved into exactly the right position. Your position in Christ opens the door for you to bask in unparalleled, limitless, freedom-filled living. In Him, your life and work have every possibility of being God-directed, Spirit-empowered, purpose-filled, and immensely satisfying. The potential is there for you to experience true joy and walk in the fullness of His plans and purposes daily. When you place yourself in God's hands, He will free you from the confines of your past and lead you into the land of promise. Cage life will no longer be your reality!

Is it really possible to discover and experience God's plans and purposes for our daily lives and work? According to Byron it is.

When he attended the Life Purpose Workshop, Byron chose red because it was his favorite color. His sole reason for being there, or so he thought, was to show support for his wife and daughters who were attending. But by the end of the workshop, Byron knew he was there for himself. Learning God's truths about his daily life and work was the start of a journey that dramatically altered the course of his life.

Byron has always been a hands-on person. He built a child's version of a television set when he was seven. As a teen, he helped his father build two houses. In all of his married life, his wife has only called a repairman once and that was because the refrigerator was still under warranty. Everything else that needed fixing, Byron fixed. But fixing things wasn't enough. Byron believed he had to do more.

As a young man, Byron obtained a degree in music and spent seventeen years playing the trumpet as a member of the local symphony orchestra. It was not surprising to learn the direction he had chosen for his life was influenced by his need for the approval of his parents and the applause of others. But playing the trumpet was not enough for Byron. He believed he had to do more.

By the time he attended the Life Purpose Workshop, Byron had made a number of career changes. He was also heavily involved in ministry at his local church. Yet Byron had never experienced spiritual fulfillment or the sense of significance he so strongly desired. His efforts were never enough; he believed he had to do more.

Today, after learning God's truths and applying them to his life, Byron is working at a custom woodworking shop in the Rocky Mountains of Colorado. Woodworking is his full-time ministry. Every piece of furniture he builds is a testament to God's design for his life.

From tools...to trumpet...and back to the tools he loved as a child. Byron now knows that devoting himself to God to complete the work He prepared in advance for him is more than enough.

CHAPTER TWO

Work Through the Eyes of God
God's Original Design for Work

"To You I lift up my eyes, O You who are
enthroned in the heavens!"
—PSALM 123:1 (NAS)

Once you have discovered that the majority of people are dissatisfied with their worklife and you understand the cause for their dissatisfaction, you may have a greater understanding of the frustration you feel in your own life. You may also have a greater awareness of the spiritual longing expressed by your family members, friends, and co-workers. Similar to Byron before he attended the workshop, your need for spiritual fulfillment and connection remains unmet in spite of your sincere efforts to serve God.

Gaining an eternal perspective is critical to completing the work God has prepared for you. When you have an eternal perspective, it helps you understand that your everyday life and work are part of God's overarching plans and purposes. You will come to the understanding that your work is of utmost importance to God and that it has eternal value. Today you will begin to view work through God's eyes.

In the movie *Bruce Almighty*, Jim Carrey plays a television reporter who desperately wants to be promoted to the anchorman position for the evening news. He blames God when he does not get the promotion. Bruce's image of God depicts Him as "a mean kid sitting on an anthill with a magnifying glass."

17

God responds by meeting Bruce face-to-face and empowering him to experience life from God's perspective. Initially, Bruce misuses the position God grants him. Taking revenge on his 'enemies', he ends up creating total chaos. Bruce's image of God changes in the midst of this chaos. So does his image of himself and his work.

Bruce kneels down in desperation on a highway at the movie's end and cries out to God, "You win. I'm done. I don't want to do this anymore. I want You to decide what's right for me. I surrender to Your will."

Finding himself in heaven because "you can't kneel down in the middle of a highway and live to talk about it, son," God tells Bruce, "You have the divine spark. You have the gift for bringing joy and laughter to the world. I know. I created you."

Bruce returns to earth and joyfully resumes his job as a reporter of humorous news stories, exactly the place where his God-given talents are put to their best use. He now has a more accurate 'picture' of who God is and how God designed him for work.

Similar to Bruce, each of us carries a mental image of God. I heard a story about a little girl who gathered her crayons and paper to draw a picture. When asked by her mother, "What are you going to draw?" the little girl replied, "I am drawing a picture of God." "But," her mother responded, "nobody knows what God looks like." To which the little girl replied, "Well, they will when I'm done!"

Take a moment to examine your mental picture of God. What do you see Him doing? Is He sitting on His throne, ruling? Does your image of God include Him 'working' and 'doing'? Does it show He is intimately involved in your daily activities to accomplish His plans and purposes? Or do you feel, as Bruce felt, that God is responsible for your unhappiness or lack of promotion?

The Bible clearly reveals many of the things we imagine about God and eternity are simply not true. You may envision eternity to be a place of unending rest and relaxation. But eternity is definitely not the inactivity of laying on white sandy beaches or the cartoon picture of endlessly playing a harp while floating on a big puffy cloud. For those of us who like being actively purposeful, physical, and relational, all of which God created us to be, the thought of eternal inactivity bores us to the point of preferring life on earth rather than in heaven!

Eternity defies description. However, God does not leave us without some insightful glimpses into the heavenly dimension where time does not exist. Without knowing everything there is to know about heaven, we can identify some characteristics that have a relevant message for us today.

Come with me to the heavenly realm. *Join* me as we experience a working God. *Learn* with me as we watch a real-life drama, as presented in the Scriptures. *Take* a seat and *observe* God and the angels at work in the eternal kingdom. The scenes you will see hold truth for each one of us. The drama portrayed is like none other because it will change how you view your daily life and work. You will learn that work is integral to the nature of God and His creation. You will be given a taste of God's plan for your work, and you will find it tastes good—really good.

SCENE ONE: CREATION IN THE PRESENCE OF GOD

As we open the Bible to the first book, Genesis, meaning 'The Beginning', we find ourselves ushered into our drama. The setting is God's workroom in eternity.

We see God at work, involved in the grand creation of the earth and the universe. The environment is full of activity, but it is not the stress-filled pace that often accompanies our days. It is purposeful, productive, stress-free work. Purpose fills the air as God the Father, Jesus Christ the Son, the Holy Spirit, and the angelic beings fulfill their individual work responsibilities. Heaven is filled with plans and purposes. No one languishes here. Boredom is unknown. Laziness is unheard of. Mindless activity? Never. Only purpose-directed work.

We watch in amazement as the Trinity—the Father, the Son, and the Holy Spirit—work. We see in this drama that God is one, yet three. We observe each person in the Godhead working together to perform different work responsibilities to fulfill the plans and purposes of God.

We watch with great anticipation as the Father steps forward to fulfill His unique role. Actively present in creation, He is the Administrator of the Universe, the Overseer, and Judge. The Father's role is revealed in many different verses throughout the Bible.

- Psalm 7:11a describes God as a Judge. *"God is a righteous judge..."* A judge is a magistrate, a person in charge.

- In Psalm 44:4, God issues decrees. *"You are my King and my God, who decrees victories for Jacob."* Decree means to rule, order, or declare. This passage reveals God the Father rules the universe, ordering the sun, moon, and stars.

- Psalm 45:6 tells us God is on the throne and that He will be there forever. *"Your throne, O God, will last for ever and ever;..."* The meaning in this verse is that He is 'Chief'.

The Father oversees all events from the eternal realm. He established and administers the laws that govern our universe and our lives. He is the Leader of the Godhead.

Is work part of God's eternal plans and purposes? It must be. As we have seen, the Father is at work in the heavens. His work is ongoing and continues today. But what about the Son? Is He working?

Let's return to our drama as Jesus Christ, Son of God, steps forward to fulfill His unique work assignments given to Him by the Father. Jesus' work is to carry out God's 'building program'. Thus, we see the Son portrayed as the Creator or Builder of the physical realm.

"Through him all things were made; without him nothing was made that has been made." —JOHN 1:3

An interesting picture evolves when we view Jesus' work assignments. As part of the Godhead, He created the universe from the eternal realm and then came to earth as a carpenter. He spent much of His life on earth as a craftsman—a Master Builder and Artisan. When Jesus completed His ultimate work assignment, dying on a cross, He prepared the way for the next step in God's building program—the Church. Jesus told His disciples, "On this rock I will build my church." Jesus Christ is the rock. The Church is built upon Him. Christ is our rock and our foundation. Other verses refer to Jesus as the cornerstone. A cornerstone refers to the foundation of a building, fitting perfectly into Jesus' role of Master Builder.

And the building continues. Before Jesus departed this earth, He told His disciples He was going back to the Father to prepare a place for them. Jesus, Creator of the Universe, Carpenter of Nazareth, Cornerstone of the Church, is now the Builder of mansions in Heaven:

"In My Father's house are many mansions; if it were not so, I would have told you. I go to prepare a place for you."

—JOHN 14:2 (NKJV)

Two themes stand out as we consider the work of the Son. First, His work began in eternity, stretched through time on earth, and continues into eternity. His work is never done. Second, a common thread runs through each of Jesus' work responsibilities: each contributed to the plans and purposes of the Father.

So, is work a part of God's eternal plans and purposes? Absolutely. The Father and the Son are very much at work in the eternal realm and on earth. But what about the Holy Spirit? He, too, is a worker.

Re-entering our drama, we see the Holy Spirit actively at work. His is the work of mediation. As the go-between or intermediary, He mediates between the invisible spiritual realm and the visible physical realm. His role is the 'breathing' of life, the giving and understanding of God's wisdom and power. We see this demonstrated in the garden.

"Then the Lord God formed a man from the dust of the ground and breathed into his nostrils the breath of life, and the man became a living being." —GENESIS 2:7

When God breathed the breath of life into Adam, the Holy Spirit entered and Adam became alive to God. We see this same truth in the New Testament when Jesus breathed the breath of life into His disciples:

"And with that he breathed on them and said, 'Receive the Holy Spirit.'" —JOHN 20:22

Clearly the Holy Spirit brings life and renews our spirit. He is the one who makes us alive to God. The Holy Spirit, the Breath of Life.

The Holy Spirit's work as Mediator between God and man is never finished. He is continuously available to help us know God. He reveals God's plans and purposes to mankind. Throughout Scripture, we see the Holy Spirit in the role of Counselor—or Helper—and Teacher:

"But the Helper, the Holy Spirit, whom the Father will send in My name, He will teach you all things, and bring to your remembrance all that I said to you." —JOHN 14:26 (NAS)

John 16:7 (NAS) also affirms the Holy Spirit is our Helper:

"But I tell you the truth, it is to your advantage that I go away; for if I do not go away, the Helper will not come to you; but if I go, I will send Him to you."

When Jesus departed, He did not leave us alone. He sent the Holy Spirit to reveal the truth, to counsel us in the ways of God.

The Bible reveals the work of the Holy Spirit is centered on the primary role of Mediator. As intermediary between the invisible realm and the physical realm, He:

* Inspires wisdom, understanding, knowledge, and strength (Exodus 31:1–6; Isaiah 11:2; Job 32:8)

* Revitalizes our hearts (Jeremiah 31:31–34)

* Baptizes believers (Luke 3:22)

* Convicts us of sin (John 16:8)

* Guides us in truth (John 16:13)

Throughout eternity, the Holy Spirit continues to work alongside the rest of the Godhead. God the Father, Administrator and Judge; Jesus the Son, Artisan, Master Builder; and the Holy Spirit, Comforter, Counselor, Helper, and Teacher, work in harmony to fulfill God's unending plans and purposes. But is there more to the drama?

Return with me to the main stage on which we saw the Trinity at work. Surrounding God, we see His workers, the angels. Depicted in biblical references as unique in appearance, angels also have unique personalities and abilities. Differences in rank are observable among the angels; some are more powerful than others. In Daniel 10:12-13, we listen in as an angel, sent by God, talks with Daniel.

"Then he continued, 'Do not be afraid, Daniel. Since the first day that you set your mind to gain understanding and to humble

24

yourself before your God, your words were heard, and I have come in response to them. But the prince of the Persian kingdom resisted me twenty-one days. Then Michael, one of the chief princes, came to help me, because I was detained there with the king of Persia.'"

The Bible presents numerous portraits of the angels, but what is most pertinent is that we are told they have individual work assignments. Angels are uniquely designed by God to fulfill different responsibilities. Psalm 103:20-21 (TLB) gives a picture of the angels receiving and completing their work assignments:

"Bless the Lord, you mighty angels of his who carry out his orders, listening for his commands. Yes, bless the Lord, you armies of his angels who serve Him constantly."

As we observe the heavenly scene, angels come before the throne of God to receive their work assignments. Then we see them departing to fulfill God's commands. When their assignments are completed, they return to the throne and await their next responsibilities. What a tremendous picture—angels coming and going before the throne of God as they are dispatched to:

- Deliver answers to prayer. (Daniel 9:20–22)

- Bring God's messages to mankind. In Acts 7:53 we discover that God dispatched angels to deliver His law to Moses on Mt. Sinai.

- Protect God's people, as when Elisha and his servant saw angels surrounding them. (II Kings 6:14–17)

- Pour out the judgment of God. (Revelation, chapter 16)

We see that angels are uniquely created beings, designed to serve and glorify God throughout eternity. Angels are God's workers.

HOW HAVE WE BEEN ENLIGHTENED?

- Work began in eternity. It existed in the invisible realm long before God created the physical universe. We serve a working God.

- There is a system, or eternal kingdom economy, of work. God the Father, Jesus the Son, the Holy Spirit, and the angels actively participate in God's eternal kingdom work.

- God is one, yet He is three Persons. He is a Trinity. Each Being in the Godhead performs a unique role. Each One's work is consistent with that role.

- Angels are uniquely created to serve and glorify God forever through the work assignments they are given by the Father.

The images of the Father, the Son, the Holy Spirit, and the angels working together in the eternal realm are firmly planted in our hearts and minds. We wish we could remain forever, but the curtain slowly draws to a close.

CHAPTER THREE

Garden Work

God's Original Design for Mankind

"Now the LORD God had planted a garden in the east, in Eden; and there he put the man he had formed." —GENESIS 2:8

Now that we understand the Godhead has individual work assignments, we will discover that mankind does as well. Creation mirrors the Creator.

Return with me to God's eternal workroom. Center stage is Adam, contentedly working. Designed by the Creator to participate in the garden work surrounding him, Adam is secure in his environment and intimacy with God. Having received his assignments directly from the Creator, he instinctively knows exactly what to do. Living and working for God, Adam is filled with purpose as he sets out each morning, anticipating another great day. After all, everything he does is meaningful and a gift of service to his Creator.

Adam spends the day caring for the garden. Variety and challenge characterize his responsibilities. Adam readily acknowledges his work is delightful, fulfilling, and 'right up his alley'. He 'wraps up' at the end of each day with a sense of satisfaction and fulfillment. He knows his Creator will guide him in his next steps when they meet for their daily walk. Adam also knows God will say, "Well done."

Why would God have debuted mankind with work? This action of God must be part of an underlying principle, best understood in light of whom the Creator is—a working God.

Feel with Adam the deep contentment in his accomplishments at each day's end. Adam knows and experiences true success: *bringing glory to God on earth by completing the work He gave him to do*—*w*ork that fit with *whom* God created Adam to be.

God's intent is for Adam to have dominion over the earth— to be empowered with the Holy Spirit and reign and rule with God forever. Imagine a lifetime of fulfillment in the garden, walking and talking with God, reigning and ruling with Him forever. Consider this verse:

"...rule over the fish of the sea and over the birds of the sky and over every living thing that moves on the earth."

—GENESIS 1:28b (NAS)

This sequence of events shows us that work is *not* a product of the Fall but has always been a vital part of God's plans and purposes. Adam's work is a natural extension of God's eternal work. It is a system of work that has always existed, beginning and ending with God.

Figure 1 shows the earth is seated in eternity and is an integral part of God's eternal kingdom economy. The arrow indicates God extended His kingdom work into the physical dimension when He created the earth.

KINGDOM WORK

Figure 1

Adam lived and worked in the physical world. Separation from God was unknown. Just as the angels' work in the invisible realm was service to God, Adam's work in the physical realm was valued service to God.

Why would God choose to create the physical world? Why not just create mankind and let him live and work in the invisible realm? While we cannot know all of God's reasons behind His actions, perhaps His action flowed out of a desire to have a different type of being who could reign and rule with Him.

*"When I consider your heavens, the work of your fingers, the moon and the stars, which you have set in place, what is mankind that you are mindful of them, human beings that you care for them? You have made them a little lower than the angels and crowned them with glory and honor. You made them rulers over the works of your hands; you put everything under their feet: all flocks and herds, and the animals of the wild, the birds in the sky, and the fish in the sea, all that swim the paths of the seas." —*PSALM 8:3–8

A picture of God's kingdom of work emerges when we take a closer look at Adam's work. In fact, Adam's life in the garden is a magnificent case study of God's original intent for mankind's work. Let's look at some of the qualities and characteristics of Adam's garden work.

ADAM WAS ALIVE TO GOD

Adam's garden work involved every aspect of his being—body, soul, and spirit. Total harmony existed among each of these different aspects of Adam's makeup. Adam instinctively knew the richness of work in God's service. Every day of his life represented a fresh opportunity to experience God as the vital director of life and work.

ADAM WORKED FOR GOD

We can think of God as Adam's 'Human Resource Manager' because God gave him his job assignments directly. Adam was in the service of the King of kings, and God was his Manager or Administrator. Adam listened to God's instructions and carried out each of his assignments with gladness. Drudgery was unknown; insignificance was non-existent.

ADAM'S WORK WAS HIS SPIRITUAL ACT OF WORSHIP

God did not create the Church of Eden so Adam could attend a worship service once a week. He put Adam in the garden to serve and worship his Creator *daily* through his work. Caring for the garden and naming the animals were acts of reverence and adoration to God. It was Adam's full-time ministry. Daily life and work were one fantastic worship service! There was no separation between work and worship. Adam did not define certain parts of his work as ministry and others as secular. He had never heard of secular work. It was beyond his scope of experience. Work without God? What was that?

Living and working in the kingdom economy, Adam did things the kingdom way. In a manner as natural as breathing, he offered up all he did as a gift to his Creator.

ADAM WAS FILLED WITH ETERNAL PURPOSE

A former USA Today survey asked adults what one question they would like to ask God or a Supreme Being. The majority responded that they would ask, "What's my purpose here?" Imagine what would happen if USA Today were to ask Adam this same question. Adam would wonder if the reporter was out of his mind. After all, he talked to his Creator daily and Adam knew exactly why he was placed in the garden. His purpose was to glorify God through his care of the garden. Lack of purpose was not Adam's problem.

ADAM RECEIVED HIS ASSIGNMENTS DIRECTLY FROM GOD

Adam's work assignments were ready for him long before he was ready for them.   Before Adam arrived on the scene, God created the garden. In doing so, He established the pattern for man's work. First, God prepares the work. Then, He designs the person for the work and reveals the work that precisely fits with that person's design. The work and the worker intricately fit with God's preordained plan.

ADAM'S MOTIVE WAS PURE

Adam carried out his assignments with purity in this spiritually vibrant relationship. He had no ulterior motive. Resting secure in the knowledge of his purpose and experiencing the joy of serving God, he had no need to seek God's approval. He did not try to advance his position or gain personal recognition. Adam knew he already had God's favor, so he had no need to work to gain it. Their relationship was saturated with love and acceptance.

ADAM WAS OBEDIENT TO GOD

Secure in his relationship, Adam didn't question God about the work He had given him. Adam carried out his work assignments with joy when God revealed them. It was that simple. Most of us are not familiar with this type of obedience, but it is a distinguishing mark of the way things worked in the garden.

ADAM WAS EMPOWERED AND EDUCATED BY GOD

Consider how Adam obtained his education in preparation for his work. The Creator Himself was Adam's source of knowledge. (It does not get any better than that!) Instead of enrolling Adam in the University of Eden, God directed and equipped Adam with all he would need to complete his work assignments. Adam had specifically been designed with all of the relational capacities and all of the physical attributes of a gardener. As Author and Designer, God knew which qualities were necessary. He designed Adam to complete his work effectively and He gave him the Holy Spirit as a guide. Adam's God-given gifts and abilities were developed by completing the work assignments given to him by God. Each assignment was designed to further his knowledge and develop his talents for the next assignment.

ADAM SAW ONLY THE POSSIBILITIES

The circumstances into which Adam was placed knew no limits. The possibilities were endless. Unlike the polar bear in Chapter One, Adam was not limited by physical circumstances or shortsightedness. He was set to soar. Phrases such as 'I can't do this because...' never found their way into Adam's vocabulary. For Adam, the garden represented his sphere of influence and authority. Knowing God had created him to reign and rule over the garden, Adam functioned effectively in his position of authority. He was, in fact, the most influential creature in the garden, reigning and ruling over the fish, plants, and animals. (Reference Genesis 2:15; Psalm 8:3–8)

ADAM'S PROVISION WAS FROM GOD

Adam understood a basic principle that seems to elude our modern minds. Adam did not work for provision. He knew God was his Provider, and therefore he trusted God for *all* his provision. God, on the other hand, freely provided Adam with all he needed. This is an important principle because it is vital to understanding God's plans and purposes for our own lives. Adam did not work to earn provision or to put food on the table. God freely provided for his needs. Adam intimately knew God, and he offered his work freely to Him as an act of worship without thought of a paycheck. Adam was a very rich man.

Let's summarize the principle elements of God's original intent for work as showcased in Adam's life in the garden:

- Adam was alive to God.

- Adam worked for God.

- Adam's work was his spiritual act of worship.

- Adam was filled with eternal purpose.

- Adam received his assignments directly from God.

- Adam's motive was pure.

- Adam was obedient to God.

- Adam was empowered and educated by God.

- Adam saw only the possibilities.

- Adam's provision was from God.

A story from Butch's life illustrates how these principles can be applied to our lives today.

Butch grew up on a farm in Queen Creek, Arizona. He attended the University of Arizona and graduated with a marketing degree. His major goal in life was to make a lot of money. He expected to accomplish this through his degree and by working for a major corporation. Following graduation, Butch joined the military, where he experienced the ultimate in 'corporate' living. Realizing corporate life was not for him, he decided he would be able to make more money, more quickly, farming with his dad on his father's 1,200-acre potato farm.

When he started working on the farm, Butch was put in charge of field operations and machinery. His father, an inventor at heart, had made three machines to harvest potatoes, which, when working, could replace seventy field workers. The problem was that the machines did not work very often.

Butch had accepted Christ as his personal Savior when he was a young man, but he didn't fully comprehend how to serve God through his work. When he began working on the farm, the thought came to him, "Commit this potato harvest to God. If you do it will be a witness to your father, it will be the best harvest he has ever had and it will confirm that God cares about your work." After seeking counsel from a pastor and praying about it, Butch committed the potato harvest to God.

Ideas for improving the efficiency of his father's machines 'came' to Butch when he was working on them. He realized these thoughts had to be from God. Butch redesigned the machines so one machine was capable of doing the work of his father's three original machines.

The machine worked so well during the harvest that fewer workers were needed. Whereas the original machines ran so slowly that workers were able to walk alongside them, the newly improved harvester moved so quickly that workers had to run to keep up with it. This resulted in an overall 70 % savings in field costs.

Butch's father came to him on the final day of the harvest and said, "Son, this is the best potato harvest we have ever had." This confirmed what God had previously revealed to Butch: "It will be a witness to your father, it will be the best harvest he has ever had, and it will confirm that God cares about your work." Butch now knew beyond a doubt that God cared deeply about his work.

CHAPTER FOUR

Paradise Lost

Secular Work Is Birthed

*"Therefore, just as through one man sin entered into the
world, and death through sin, and so death spread to all men,
because all sinned—"* —ROMANS 5:12 (NAS)

Created to live and work to contribute to God's eternal plans
and purposes—what a marvelous revelation! Yet, we need only
look at our own lives to realize something occurred that altered
the course of human history.

One word says it all: disobedience—a disregard for God's
commandments and a life-changing choice to 'do things my
way'. A description of this is found in Genesis 3:12–14a; 17–19:

*"The man said, 'The woman you put here with me—she gave me
some fruit from the tree, and I ate it.' Then the LORD God said
to the woman, 'What is this you have done?' The woman said,
'The serpent deceived me, and I ate.' So the LORD God said to
the serpent, 'Because you have done this, cursed are you above
all livestock and all wild animals! ... To Adam he said, 'Because
you listened to your wife and ate fruit from the tree about which I
commanded you, "You must not eat from it," Cursed is the
ground because of you; through painful toil you will eat food
from it all the days of your life. It will produce thorns and thistles
for you, and you will eat the plants of the field. By the sweat of
your brow you will eat your food until you return to the ground,*

since from it you were taken; for dust you are and to dust you will return.'"

And with that, life changed. Adam and Eve were cast from the garden, and the entrance was sealed. Adam lost his coveted position. Though he was still the caretaker of the earth, perfect communion with God was broken, and garden life was no longer Adam's reality. Sin now separated man and the earth from God.

Figure 2 provides a visual representation of the consequences of Adam's disobedience. Notice a shroud of sin separates mankind and the earth from God. Created to be a vibrant part of God's eternal kingdom economy, the earth is now cut off from eternity and all things have become temporal.

Figure 2

Another illustration of this same truth, shown in Figure 3, would be a bridge. On one side of the bridge we see God's kingdom economy of work into which Adam was originally created. Cast from the garden, the devastating result for Adam,

Eve, and all mankind thereafter was that we were moved across the bridge into the newly birthed secular world economy of work. Notice the chasm that separates God's kingdom work from the newly birthed secular work.

Figure 3

We are all subject to the consequences of the Fall. Cage life is one of the consequences, but there are others. Let's consider some of the other characteristics of life and work in the secular world economy.

MAN DIED SPIRITUALLY

When Adam disobeyed God the result was spiritual death. Created with three equally valuable aspects to his being—physical, relational, and spiritual—Adam's spiritual aspect died to God when he ate from the forbidden tree of the knowledge of good and evil. The result was that an unnatural phenomenon was birthed—secular work. For the first time in human history, man's work was cut off from God. With Adam's separation from God, the spiritual death toll rang on all men and women born thereafter. We have all been born empty of the Spirit of God since the Fall.

Work without God—secular work—has temporal value. It contributes to the well-being of the earth and mankind; however, secular work has no eternal value. It is not a part of the kingdom economy. What we experience daily in the world is a cheap imitation of what God intended. It is a hollow look-alike of the original plan for God-focused, deeply satisfying work.

WE WORK FOR OURSELVES INSTEAD OF GOD

The world economy functions opposite from God's kingdom economy. Serving ourselves and seeking to please man instead of God, our lives are self-focused and soul emptying. We accept work as drudgery and try to find fulfillment and significance through other avenues. The fact that as many as 81% of all workers are dissatisfied with their work life reveals that our reality is the Fall. Failing to recognize that secular work is contrary to God's original intention, cage life has become the norm.

WORK AND WORSHIP ARE NO LONGER THE SAME

God intended work to be an act of worship. When we confuse the Sunday service with all that worship is meant to be, we become spiritual paupers. God intended us to glorify Him on a daily basis. Worship is not limited to Sundays. When we pay homage to God and show our devotion to Him through our daily lives and work, we are living out the true meaning of worship.

This is how Adam approached his work, and it brought him fulfillment. In a manner as natural as breathing, Adam offered up all he did as a gift to his Creator. After the Fall, work became burdensome to Adam and 'sweat of the brow' work became a harsh reality. The delightful fulfilling work God intended to be an act of worship for Adam ended.

Many people believe work became burdensome because God cursed it. This is untrue. God did not curse work. Adam was doing God's work; therefore, cursing Adam's work would have been equivalent to God cursing His own work. Genesis 3:17-19 tells us that God cursed the ground; there is no record of God ever having cursed work.

"...Cursed is the ground because of you; through painful toil you will eat food from it all the days of your life. It will produce thorns and thistles for you, and you will eat the plants of the field. By the sweat of your brow you will eat your food until you return to the ground, since from it you were taken; for dust you are and to dust you will return."

WE STRUGGLE TO FIND SIGNIFICANCE

Living and working for God, Adam was filled with eternal purpose as he set out each morning, anticipating another great day. After all, everything he did was meaningful and ultimately a gift of service to his Creator.

After the Fall, eternity was no longer his reality and it is no longer ours. We struggle to find significance and lasting value in our daily lives and work. While we may recognize we are making a contribution, the sense of purpose Adam experienced in the garden has been lost.

WE LOOK FOR JOBS THROUGH MAN-MADE AVENUES

Many people have experienced the frustrations of searching for a job—updating their resumes, reading the want ads, looking at job listings on the Internet. Contrast this with how Adam received his assignments in the garden. Instead of conducting a job search, he relied on God to reveal the work He had prepared for him. In the world economy, we no longer believe God works in this same way.

As Christians, we may like to believe prayer is an integral part of this process. Yet when I facilitated the Life Purpose Workshop I did not find this to be the case. When I asked people how they found work, only one person over a ten-year time frame mentioned prayer and it was an afterthought at that. When I asked participants to list all of the ways people find jobs, one woman said, "We probably should have added prayer to the list." The reality for many of us is that we conduct a job search on our own and then ask God to bless us after we have found the job we thought we wanted. This is a sad commentary on how far we have fallen from God's ways.

WE ARE MOTIVATED TO SERVE OURSELVES

Adam's motivation in the garden was to serve and glorify God. We view work in the world economy as an opportunity to serve and glorify ourselves. Attempting to better our positions, we often engage in work that no longer fits with our God-given talents. We put greater emphasis on 'climbing the corporate ladder' and increasing the size of our paycheck than serving our Creator.

WE ARE DISOBEDIENT TO GOD

When Adam was in the garden he was secure in his relationship with God. He was secure because obedience to God was his modus operandi. He received his assignments from God and completed them without question. Obedience does not come through evaluating an assignment, deciding if it is the one we want, and then doing it. Biblical obedience is completing each assignment without question. The biblical definition of the word *obedience* contains a sense of immediacy. It can be described through the example of a knock at the door. When we hear a knock, we stop what we are doing and simply respond by answering the door.

Disobedience became the norm after the Fall. Man became more interested in 'doing his own thing' instead of doing things God's way. When we consider our own situations, do we listen for His 'knock' so we can respond immediately? Or do we rush out the door each day, arranging our activities and schedules on the basis of our own personal needs and desires? Is God even part of our equation as it pertains to daily life and work?

WE RELY ON MAN-MADE EDUCATION AND PERSONAL EXPERIENCE

In the world economy education and experience are considered the gateway to success and the means by which we better ourselves. Adam was directly educated by God in the garden. Each assignment was designed to prepare him for the next task.

When we subscribe to the belief that education and experience are the sure steppingstones to a bright unlimited future, we are subscribing to Satan's lie. Paul, never a man to mince words, put it this way in Philippians 3:8 (NAS):

"More than that, I count all things to be loss in view of the surpassing value of knowing Christ Jesus my Lord, for whom I have suffered the loss of all things, and count them but rubbish so that I may gain Christ."

Paul knew his privilege and secular education could open the doors to his temporal future but never to eternity. When wrongly motivated, education is of no lasting value and can lead to a career where we are unfulfilled and left wondering what went wrong. In light of this, it is important to know one's calling *before* making educational decisions.

WE SEE ROADBLOCKS

The world's system creates roadblocks. Education and experience can actually become barriers that prevent us from moving beyond our secular mindset into the fullness of God's plans and purposes for our lives. This can be recognized through the way we look for jobs. While many of us may have a desire to move into a different area of work that is more fulfilling and would be a better fit with our God-given talents, we are often reluctant to do so. Our unwillingness comes from the fact that 'cage life', although wearisome, brings a sense of security. Having invested so much time and energy in our career paths, we are hesitant to take the risk that comes with making a change. Instead of seeing the limitless possibilities in Christ, we see only the roadblocks.

The truth is that, for most of us, if we were to lose our jobs today, we would look for exactly the same type of work we have been doing—work that fits with our experience and education. Our self-imposed roadblocks convince us we are not capable of moving in a different direction to pursue our God-given destiny.

WE WORK TO EARN A PAYCHECK

Work replaces God as Provider in the world economy. We rely on a paycheck instead of on God for provision. We elevate self-sufficiency to a virtue, not realizing how far we have strayed from God's original plan. Having taken the privilege of provision from God, we burden ourselves with a responsibility for which we were never designed. While God may choose to provide for us through a paycheck, provision comes in many forms and it is intended to be a free gift from God. Adam did not work for provision in the garden.

How easy it is for us to lose sight of these truths, as Butch did when his father sold the farm ten years after the successful potato harvest. Not knowing what else to do, Butch accepted a position with his local church. For the next three years he oversaw and maintained the church camp. When the need for a new dormitory was recognized, Butch received construction training from a friend who was a general contractor. This eventually led to his career in contracting.

During the years Butch worked at the church and in general contracting, he never lost his desire to make a lot of money. Forgetting the lessons he had learned on the farm, Butch transitioned from general contracting to building speculative homes to commercial development, with a drive to make more and more money. Each decision took him further away from God's design for his daily life and work and eventually led him down the path of financial ruin. It was at this point in his life that we met and Butch began the journey of recommitting his work to God.

TWO ECONOMIES OF WORK CONTRASTED

Clearly everything changed when Adam disobeyed God. A page in history was turned. The perfect harmony between God and man was broken. Work 'by the sweat of your brow' became our reality. We need only review the contrast between the two economies of work on page 47 to gain understanding of why we experience the emptiness of the secular and struggle to discover the significance of the eternal.

World Economy	Kingdom Economy
Man died spiritually	*Adam was alive to God*
We work for ourselves instead of God	*Adam worked for God*
Work and worship are no longer the same	*Adam's work was his spiritual act of worship*
We struggle to find significance	*Adam was filled with eternal purpose*
We look for jobs through man-made avenues	*Adam received his assignments directly from God*
We are motivated to serve ourselves	*Adam's motive was pure*
We are disobedient to God	*Adam was obedient to God*
We rely on man-made education and personal experience	*Adam was empowered and educated by God*
We see roadblocks	*Adam saw only the possibilities*
We work to earn a paycheck	*Adam's provision was from God*

By now you may find yourself thinking, "Why bother? If the Fall is our reality, how can we expect anything different?" The good news is that God loves us, and He does not leave us without hope. He uniquely created us, and He yearns to fulfill His plans and purposes for our daily lives and work. That is why

He sent his Son, Jesus Christ to die on the cross to save us from our sins and restore what had been lost through the Fall.

Janne gained insight into the power of His shed blood through the recent bone marrow transplant of her brother. Janne received a call from her older brother, Tony, in September 2012. He had just been diagnosed with leukemia. For treatment, it was necessary that his siblings be tested to see if they would be a match for him to receive a bone-marrow transplant through the donation of blood stem cells. When the results of the blood work and the DNA testing came back, it revealed that Janne was a perfect match.

Before flying to Minnesota, Janne pondered the reality that she could say, "No." Submitting herself and her body to this treatment plan was not something she had to do. The procedure would require six days of injections to increase her white blood cell count, with possible side effects. On the fifth and sixth days of the injections, a needle would be inserted into her right arm for approximately six hours to draw the blood. It would then be spun through a machine to separate the needed stem cells while a needle in her other arm would return her blood back to her body.

As she thought this through, she questioned what it was that made her agree to all of this. The answer was love. Love for her brother and love for God. Immediately, a picture of Christ on the cross came to her mind and she heard God's still, small voice say, "That is what kept me on the cross for you."

As God used Janne's perfectly matched blood to bring health and healing back to her brother, Jesus Christ's blood is the perfect match for each one of us. Even as Tony's blood was 'contaminated' by cancer, our blood is 'contaminated' by sin.

God used a physical transfusion, through a medical procedure, to replace Tony's cancer-riddled blood with healthy blood. He uses a spiritual transfusion, through His divine procedure, to replace our sin-riddled blood with Christ's pure blood. All because of Love.

CHAPTER FIVE

God's Trademark
Grace Redefined

"THE SPIRIT OF THE LORD IS UPON ME, BECAUSE HE ANOINTED ME TO PREACH THE GOSPEL TO THE POOR. HE HAS SENT ME TO PROCLAIM RELEASE TO THE CAPTIVES, AND RECOVERY OF SIGHT TO THE BLIND, TO SET FREE THOSE WHO ARE OPPRESSED, ... "
—LUKE 4:18 (NAS)

Poor, captive, blind, and oppressed. How many of us would admit this is how we often feel? Poor because we are unfulfilled and discontent. Captive because we feel stuck in our present situation. Blind because we are not discerning God's truths regarding our daily lives and work. Oppressed because we sense we were created for more than we are experiencing.

Fortunately, God was not content to leave us there. He sent His Son, Jesus Christ, to die on the cross to provide the way for us to participate in His eternal plans and purposes for our daily lives and work. Jesus came to restore what had been lost through the Fall. Figure 4 presents a visual representation of what Jesus accomplished through His death on the cross. Notice the shroud of sin that surrounded the earth at the Fall has been pierced.

Figure 4

In Christ, we are no longer a part of this world, no longer controlled by the power of sin. We become seated with Him in God's eternal kingdom economy at the moment of our salvation. God's Word affirms this in Ephesians 2:1–6 (NAS).

"And you were dead in your trespasses and sins, in which you formerly walked according to the course of this world, according to the prince of the power of the air, of the spirit that is now working in the sons of disobedience. Among them we too all formerly lived in the lusts of our flesh, indulging the desires of the flesh and of the mind, and were by nature children of wrath, even as the rest. But God, being rich in mercy, because of His great love with which He loved us, even when we were dead in our transgressions, made us alive together with Christ (by grace you have been saved), and raised us up with Him, and seated us with Him in the heavenly places in Christ Jesus, ... "

Let's revisit the bridge illustration to enhance our understanding of this important biblical truth. When we enter into a relationship with Jesus Christ something happens. Notice the direction of the arrow in figure 5 is now pointing toward God's eternal kingdom economy, demonstrating that Christ provided the way back.

Figure 5

God's grace at the moment of our salvation moves us back across the bridge from the world economy into His eternal kingdom economy. As children of the King and members of His Royal Priesthood, we are fully positioned in God's economy—the same eternal kingdom economy in which Adam lived and worked before the Fall. The same benefits that were available to Adam in the garden are now available to us.

EXPERIENCING KINGDOM LIFE IS A PROCESS

We are positioned in God's eternal kingdom economy at the time of our salvation. Yet, being *positioned* in His economy and *experiencing* life there are two entirely different matters. Although God has positioned us in His kingdom, few of us are experiencing the rewards of living and working there. This is demonstrated through the statistics that I shared stating 81% of all people, including Christians, are dissatisfied with their work. If we are truly positioned in God's economy, why does our experience not align with our position?

The problem is that we have a lifetime of experience living and working in the world economy but almost no experience in the kingdom economy. Sadly, we are much more attuned to man's ways than God's ways. Many do not know two economies exist. Nor do many understand that the door to God's economy has been opened to those who have a relationship with Jesus Christ.

We have falsely believed that we have no choice but to operate in the world economy. Deceived into thinking work has been cursed, we subscribe to the belief that work is a platform for sharing our faith or a means to a paycheck. The result is that we lack fulfillment and significance for our daily lives.

Experiencing life and work in God's economy necessitates yielding to God in obedience (answering the 'knock') and moving experientially across the bridge. When we do this, God's eternal system of work increasingly becomes our reality.

Before Butch and I met, I was working at a large electronics company where I was responsible for supervising the computer center. Unfortunately, the computers kept breaking down. The breakdowns were just long enough for a repairman to come in, hear the Word of God from me, repair the equipment and then leave. Over the course of several months, three different repairmen came in. All three left knowing Jesus Christ as their Savior.

As a new Christian, I could not contain my joy at knowing the Lord and I frequently went into the computer room alone to sing praises to God as I worked. That is what I was doing the day I was waiting for the first repairman. Unbeknownst to me, Dan had already arrived. I was taken by surprise when I turned around and saw that he was in the computer room listening to me sing. I immediately stopped but he asked me to continue because he said he was enjoying it. (That is a story in and of itself because I cannot carry a tune!) Before the end of the day, Dan told me he wanted to experience the same joy he saw in me and asked how he could do that. As soon as he heard the truth of the gospel, he accepted Jesus Christ as his personal Savior.

The second repairmen, Bob, overheard me during my break, arranging to attend Bible study that evening and asked if he could go with me. A few days later he asked if he could talk to me. He was upset. He wanted to accept Jesus as his Savior but was having trouble finishing his list. "List?" I asked? "What list?" It turns out that he had been writing a list of all of his sins so he could confess them to Jesus but he couldn't remember them all. What a relief it was for him when I explained that Jesus already knew his sins and He forgave them all as soon as Bob confessed his need for a Savior.

The third 'repairman' turned out to be a woman whose name was Liz. By the time she arrived, I was upset with God. My boss was beginning to think he had hired the wrong person for the job since the computers continued to break down. Until they started working again, I was determined to stick to the business at hand. God, though, had other plans.

While sitting at my desk one day, I sensed God wanted me to share my faith with Liz. "How, Lord?" I asked. "I have hardly spoken to her in three days and I don't know how to start." I asked God to arrange the situation if He wanted me to talk to her. Liz came out of the computer room within minutes and invited me to join her for lunch. I followed her into the break room and sat down. "Okay, God, what's next?" I silently asked.

About that time, Georgia, the security guard, walked into the room. She had been attending Bible study with me and wanted to hear the Word of God again. "Joanne," she said "tell me about Jesus." I quickly mumbled something but Georgia would not let me get away with that. God used her to prompt me to tell the story of Adam and Eve, the Fall, sin and death, the birth of Jesus Christ, His death on the cross, and forgiveness of our sins. Then Georgia got up and left the room as abruptly as she had entered. I, too, started to leave but Liz quickly stopped me. She wanted to know how to receive forgiveness. Liz was raised in a religion that taught you confessed your sins to a person and she had been struggling with that. Uncertain of what to believe, she had been asking God to reveal His truth. Liz accepted Jesus as her Lord and Savior that day, and, wouldn't you know, the computers started working again.

Let's take another look at the comparison between the world economy and the kingdom economy on page 47 to determine in which economy we are operating. Be advised, trials are not an indication of the economy in which we are living and working. We will experience trials as long as we are on earth. As Jesus

56

attested in John 16:33, we are not immune from the difficulties of the world:

"...In this world you will have trouble. But take heart! I have overcome the world."

The difference, for believers, is that the impact of the world system lessens as we progress across the bridge experientially. Over time, we learn to rise above our circumstances. Paul reveals this truth in Philippians 4:11 (NAS):

"... I have learned to be content in whatever circumstances I am."

Paul knew the secret of kingdom living. He chose to live God's way rather than man's.

Let's embark on the next exciting step of our journey: discovering the key to crossing the bridge into the fullness of God's plans and purposes for this life and eternity.

GRACE IS PARAMOUNT TO LIVING AND WORKING IN GOD'S ETERNAL KINGDOM ECONOMY

Grace is a vital part of God's kingdom economy. It is the key to kingdom living. This being said, we need to have a solid biblical understanding of grace. Many of us have been taught that grace refers to God's unmerited favor. We frequently use mercy and grace interchangeably; however, this is not accurate. Mercy speaks of not receiving the punishment we deserve. It is being stopped by the highway patrol because we were speeding and not being given a ticket. Mercy reveals the compassion of God. It is a good thing, but it is not grace.

The meaning of grace is profoundly deeper and broader than the bounds of unmerited favor. Grace speaks of a life-changing dimension that opens the door to God's kingdom economy. Grace *saves* us. Grace *positions* us in the kingdom economy. Grace *transforms* us into the person God created us to be. Grace *directs* us to complete the work God has prepared for us. Grace *empowers* us to experience kingdom living. Grace enables us to hear the knock.

Grace is *the empowering presence of the Holy Spirit*. It is the power of God working in us and through us. As you read the following verses, substitute *'the empowering presence of the Holy Spirit'* for the word *'grace'*.

"But by the grace of God I am what I am, and his grace to me was not without effect. No, I worked harder than all of them—yet not I, but the grace of God that was with me."

—I CORINTHIANS 15:10

"So Paul and Barnabas spent considerable time there, speaking boldly for the Lord, who confirmed the message of his grace by enabling them to perform signs and wonders." —ACTS 14:3

"You who are trying to be justified by law have been alienated from Christ; you have fallen away from grace."

—GALATIANS 5:4

"...Grace be with you." —COLOSSIANS 4:18

"The Word became flesh and made his dwelling among us. We have seen his glory, the glory of the one and only Son, who came from the Father, full of grace and truth. —JOHN 1:14

Grace—*the empowering presence of the Holy Spirit*—is at work in our hearts and minds to transform us into the people God created us to be and to complete the work He gives us to do. The Holy Spirit begins His work in us the moment we invite Jesus into our heart and He continues it until the day of our departure from this world. John 14:6 states:

"Jesus answered, 'I am the way and the truth and the life. No one comes to the Father except through me.'"

Jesus is the Door to the Father. He is the Door to the kingdom. The Holy Spirit is our Guide and Teacher. The moment we accept Jesus Christ as our Savior, the Holy Spirit moves into our hearts and takes up residence. Over time, as we make our way across the bridge by grace, the Fall is no longer our reality. As the Holy Spirit renews our hearts and minds, our work becomes our spiritual act of worship. Our need for spiritual fulfillment and connection with God is satisfied.

This is exactly what happened to Byron. Byron spent most of his life believing he had to do more. A degree in music, playing the trumpet, parental approval, applause, and a variety of careers were never enough. When he finally understood and embraced God's truths and discovered how to operate by grace, Byron experienced a paradigm shift in his thinking. By grace, Byron now knows he is enough.

God's grace is sufficient for Byron. His grace is sufficient for me…it is sufficient for you.

"But he said to me, 'My grace is sufficient for you, for my power is made perfect in weakness.'" —II CORINTHIANS 12:9a

GRACE IS A GIFT FROM GOD

Ephesians 4:1,7 (NAS) tells us that when we invite Christ into our life He gives us grace.

"...I urge you to live a life worthy of the calling you have received... But to each one of us grace has been given as Christ apportioned it."

God gives us grace in accordance with His plans and purposes, in harmony with the work He has prepared for us. This is an encouraging concept. Oswald Chambers, in his *My Utmost for His Highest*, writes: "The energy and power which was so very evident in Jesus will be exhibited in us by an act of the absolute sovereign grace of God, once we have made that complete and effective decision about sin. *'You shall receive power when the Holy Spirit has come upon you...'* (Acts 1:8)— not power as a gift from the Holy Spirit; the power *is* the Holy Spirit, not just something He gives us."

God gives us the exact amount of grace (power) we will ever need at the moment of our salvation. No one will ever have to go begging to God for a second helping of grace. Paul understood this concept—he knew that he had everything he would ever need to accomplish the work God prepared for him:

"And my God will meet all your needs according to the riches of his glory in Christ Jesus." —PHILIPPIANS 4:19

Grace is the work of a Personal Being who is willing and able to transform our lives to make kingdom life and kingdom work our daily experience. When we spend time with God and make our way across the bridge toward the kingdom economy, we will discover He has endowed us with the necessary components to accomplish the work He has prepared for us. This is exciting! It demonstrates the personal work of the Holy Spirit in each of our lives. It reveals how He empowers us, directs us, and teaches us. It reveals a purpose-filled life is a spirit-empowered life.

WE CAN DO GOD'S WORK

Doing God's work sounds good, but how is it possible? How can we experience 'garden work' when we live in the fallen secular world? As with everything that relates to kingdom living, grace is the key. If we are to do God's work, it must be done through the empowering presence of the Holy Spirit. It must be grace based. Grace-based work includes all of the God-given assignments we accomplish through the power of the Holy Spirit in our homes, neighborhoods, schools, marketplace, churches, and other religious organizations.

Grace-based work is not defined by the type of work we do but by the power source that drives it. When we yield to the Holy Spirit and the Holy Spirit accomplishes a work in and through us, God views that work as His own.

The Bible makes no distinction between the work of God, the work of Jesus Christ, the work of the Holy Spirit, the work of the angels, and the work of believers operating under grace. Regardless of where we work and regardless of the type of work we are doing, grace-based work is *always* God's work. It is our spiritual act of worship and our full-time ministry. When we operate by grace, our work stands alongside the work of God the Father, Jesus the Son, the Holy Spirit, the angels, and Adam's garden work.

Consider the implications of this long-term. If we extend the concept of grace-based work throughout the different stages of our lives, we realize, biblically speaking, that work has no end. Work may change shape or take on a different look as we age and mature, but for a believer, there should be no such thing as retirement or unemployment. Whether or not we have a paid job, we are always called to be in God's employ.

I experienced these truths firsthand. When God called me out of the corporate world in 1989 and I began working with Butch to reestablish his general contracting firm, the phone started ringing. God brought exactly the right contracting jobs to us for more than ten years. But in the spring of 2001 the phone no longer rang and the work stopped coming. It was as though God had turned off the spigot. There was no doubt we were in transition. God had another plan for us.

In August of 2001 Butch was diagnosed with cancer. There were no warning signs. He woke up one morning and could not walk. He died January 3, 2002, just four short months after his diagnosis. We had no idea this was coming, not even a hint. But God knew before the phone stopped ringing that Butch's work on earth was drawing to a close. He knew I would be so devastated by his death that I would barely be able to function. God took care of the situation in advance by shutting down the business; but, He had one last construction project for Butch prior to his death—my new home.

We had been praying for a new home for several years and had found just the right one after God closed the business. It was everything we had ever wanted—a huge shop for Butch, spacious rooms, and lots of French doors facing the large backyard with a great view of a rose garden and fruit trees.

Unaware of what lay ahead, we began an extensive remodel before Butch became ill. The remodel was finished eleven days before he died.

The sense of loss I felt after Butch died was unbearable. For months, all I could manage to do was sit in a chair and cry. The sequence of events that had transpired was beyond my comprehension. I could not understand why God had allowed this to happen. I could not imagine life without Butch. Barely able to get through a single day and uncertain of my future, God revealed that tending the rose garden was the healing work He had prepared for me.

For almost two years I tended the garden. This turned out to be one of the most beneficial seasons of my life. Gardening, for me, was a work of grace. It gave me a reason to get up in the morning. It gave me a reason to move beyond the chair that had become 'home' to me for more than seven months. Gardening was a time of healing for me. God revealed Himself to me and infused me with hope and healing through every rose petal, every seed that grew, every piece of fruit, and every shrub. In caring for the garden, I experienced God's care for me.

WHOM WILL YOU SERVE?

Through our relationship with Jesus Christ, we have been awarded citizenship in God's kingdom economy. The treasure of the Holy Spirit provides us with all of the power we will ever need to live and work there. The sad reality is, however, that we can hold citizenship in God's kingdom economy and live our entire life mired in the world economy, totally missing the target of God's will.

In the world, there is an international policy called 'extraterritoriality'. This policy provides freedom from the laws of the country in which one is living. Foreign diplomats enjoy this privilege. It gives them permission to function by the laws of their homeland and bypass those of their land of occupation.

In the spiritual realm, there is no 'extraterritoriality'. We are citizens of Heaven through our relationship with Jesus Christ and nothing can change that fact; however, the world economy is more than willing to provide us with a working visa. This creates a dilemma: we want the benefits of living and working in the kingdom economy, but we don't want to give up our position in the world.

Even though we may not find our work satisfying, the world offers us a sense of security. We receive a certain degree of comfort in knowing we will receive our paycheck on Friday; therefore, stepping onto the bridge can feed our insecurities. It can feel as though we are leaving behind everything we have ever known, including our income. Obviously, this thinking is not in line with God's truths, but it *feels* real to us. The reason this feels so real is that sin wants to keep us under the world's jurisdiction. Grace, on the other hand, wants to draw us onto the bridge.

In which economy will we live and work? Will we choose to continue under the world's jurisdiction or will we set our fears aside and step onto the bridge? Similar to the Israelites in the Old Testament, we must decide for ourselves whom we will serve this day—the god of this world or the true and living God of the Bible.

"But if serving the LORD seems undesirable to you, then choose for yourselves this day whom you will serve, whether the gods your ancestors served beyond the Euphrates, or the gods of the

Amorites, in whose land you are living. But as for me and my household, we will serve the LORD." —JOSHUA 24:15

Let's summarize the truths discussed in this chapter:

- Mercy is God's compassion. Mercy is not receiving the punishment we deserve.

- Grace is God's power. It is the empowering presence of the Holy Spirit working in us.

- God's grace, at the moment of our salvation, positions us in God's eternal kingdom economy.

- Grace is a vital part of God's kingdom economy. It is the key to kingdom living.

- Grace-based work includes all activity done through the empowering presence of the Holy Spirit. Grace-based work is *always* God's work. It is our spiritual act of worship, our full-time ministry.

Consider the benefits that come with our new position. We have the opportunity, through a relationship with Jesus Christ, to experience the fullness of God's plans and purposes every day of our lives, wherever He places us. By grace, we have the capacity, in this lifetime, on this earth, to make a contribution to eternity. Kingdom work in God's economy, as it was with Adam in the garden, can become our reality.

What does it look like and how might it feel when we are operating by grace, under the guidance of the Holy Spirit? For me, it looks and feels a lot like riding a bicycle built for two.

Butch and I took a trip to San Diego one summer and decided to go to Coronado Island and rent bicycles for the day. By the time we arrived at the rental shop there was only one bicycle left—a bicycle built for two. Having never ridden such a bicycle, I was a bit leery. But with my fearless leader in front, I hopped on the back feeling certain we would conquer the bike in no time. Was I ever wrong! We started out just fine when riding through the parking lot, but I panicked as soon as we hit traffic.

Grabbing the handlebars, I attempted to turn toward the curb to avoid a car. Nothing happened! I then grabbed the handlebars again and tugged harder. Still nothing happened! I pounded the handlebars, kicked the pedals, and screamed at Butch, "You're going to get us killed! You don't know what you're doing! Let me off!" Butch wasn't the least bit rattled. In fact, he seemed to not even listen. Eventually, after a lot of unnecessary aggravation, I got the message: I needed to sit back, relax, and trust Butch with the wheel. When I was able to do that, I enjoyed the ride.

God taught me a valuable lesson that day. I learned grace is like riding that bicycle. When we operate by grace we are allowing the Holy Spirit to take the lead, resting in the assurance He has already established our path. Over time, as we learn to relinquish control to the Holy Spirit, God's plans and purposes for us begin to unfold. The new life we are promised in Christ becomes our reality.

CHAPTER SIX

Faith Revisited

Walking by Faith, Not by Sight

*"... fixing our eyes on Jesus, the pioneer
and perfecter of faith."* — HEBREWS 12:2b

God's grace provides us with all the potential and power we will ever need to experience the fullness of His plans for us; however, *having* grace and *operating* by grace are two entirely different matters. Yielding our hearts and minds to God and being filled with the Holy Spirit does not come naturally to us in our human state. Learning to operate by grace is a process and it requires another ingredient: faith. Faith is the only way we can gain access to the grace that is within us. Romans 5:1–2 tells us:

"Therefore, since we have been justified through faith, we have peace with God through our Lord Jesus Christ, through whom we have gained access by faith into this grace in which we now stand..."

GOD GIVES US A MEASURE OF FAITH

When we accept Jesus Christ as our personal Savior, God gives us all the grace and faith we will ever need to do the work He has prepared for us. In Romans 12:3 (NAS), we learn that we have been given a measure of faith:

"For through the grace given to me I say to everyone among you not to think more highly of himself than he ought to think; but to

think so as to have sound judgment, as God has allotted to each a measure of faith."

In Christ we lack nothing. God gives us grace at the moment of our salvation and He gives us a measure of faith through which we gain access into His grace.

Grace and faith are companions. They fit together like a hand in a glove. Exercising our faith is like putting our hand into the glove. The glove is available to us but until we pick it up and put our hand into it, the glove is not activated. So it is with grace. Grace is not activated until we exercise the faith God has deposited in us.

Untapped oil reserves in sand and shale offer another illustration of this. For decades it was known that oil was encompassed in vast expanses of sand and shale, holding enough crude oil to meet years and years of energy demand. These massive energy reserves remained dormant long after they were identified because experts could not figure out how to access them. So it is with us. Not knowing how to access the reserve of grace within us, it remains largely untapped.

WE HAVE THE EXACT AMOUNT OF FAITH WE NEED

God has given each of us the exact measure of faith we need to access His grace. Our measure of faith is in perfect proportion to God's plans and purposes for us. In Christ, God has already given us all the grace and faith we will ever need to do what He calls us to do. We lack nothing.

BIBLICAL FAITH

Biblical faith is markedly different from the counterfeit faith of the secular world economy. Unlike the faith of the world system, in which we trust our employer for our paycheck at the end of the week, biblical faith trusts God to meet *all* of our needs. Biblical faith waits on God to act:

"Men have not heard nor perceived by the ear, nor has the eye seen any God besides You, Who acts for the one who waits for Him." — ISAIAH 64:4 (NKJV)

Waiting is not a popular concept in our culture, but waiting on the Lord is a critical element in our faith walk.

I had an experience about a year into my relationship with Jesus Christ that helped me understand this truth. One day, I was running behind schedule and realized my pickup truck was low on gas. Concerned about the consequences of being late for work, I knew there was no time to stop for gas. So I quickly said a prayer and forged ahead.

While driving, I saw a young man with a bicycle standing beside the road about a mile ahead of me. My truck slowed as I drew near to the bicyclist and it came to a complete stop directly in front of him. I was out of gas. Thinking I had stopped for him, the bicyclist picked up his bike and loaded it into the back of my truck. When I inquired what he was doing, he responded that his bike had a flat tire and he thought I had stopped for him. I quickly explained that I had not stopped for him but had run out of gas.

Over the next few minutes I planned my strategy. I would stand in the road, stick out my thumb, and hitchhike to the nearest gas station. The bicyclist could stay with my truck while I was getting the gas. I would purchase the gas using the station's gas can, hitchhike back to my truck, and pour the gas into the tank. Then, I would drive back to the station to return the can, take the bicyclist home, and go to work. Having it all figured out, I shared my plan with God.

As I followed through on my idea, I fully expected the first car that came by to stop. It sped by. The second car did as well. After the third car raced past me, I asked God, "What are You doing? We have a plan. I'm doing my part. You need to do your part!" Within minutes, a panel truck stopped and the driver jumped out. "Out of gas?" he asked. Then he opened the back of his panel truck to display a gas pump. The driver explained, while pumping the gas, that he owned a tree-trimming service and that it was much easier to take the gasoline to the workers than to bring the workers to the gasoline.

Before long, I was back on the road with the bicyclist happily seated in the passenger's seat. He told me he was home from a missionary trip to earn money to go back overseas. When the flat tire occurred, he had stood by the side of the road and asked God to bring a pickup truck, "Right there," indicating where the bicycle had been parked. He did not map out a plan and relay it to God. He simply asked God to meet his specific need and then waited for God to respond.

The young man followed the same strategy with the gasoline. While I was developing my grand plan and presenting it to God, he prayed and asked God to provide gasoline for my truck in whatever way God chose. He did not join me in the road with his thumb out in search of a ride; he simply prayed. The bicyclist said he had learned a long time ago that making his needs known and waiting on God was always the best solution. Situations were not always resolved on his timetable, but God had never disappointed him.

Similar to the way I had made plans to hitchhike to the gas station, it is easy to make our own plans and ask God to bless them. We call this faith. But biblical faith trusts God to meet all of our needs. Biblical faith waits on God with full assurance He will act on our behalf. God will not answer every prayer with a metaphorical gas truck but when we make our needs known to Him through prayer, He will bring the exact solution we need at exactly the right time.

Biblical faith has a dual direction. It looks upward to the Father and Jesus Christ in the heavenly realm and inward to the Holy Spirit who indwells us. Biblical faith does not function in accordance with the world. It knows no bounds. It has full confidence that the empowering presence of the Holy Spirit will work in and through us to accomplish God's plans and purposes for our daily lives and work.

When the Holy Spirit activates us for service, He provides the exact guidance we need to make our way across the bridge and complete God's work. By grace through faith, we are empowered to move forward under the Holy Spirit's direction, knowing God is at work in and through us. Nothing is impossible for Him. This is exactly why the Bible assures us that even the tiniest bit of faith—faith that is the size of a mustard seed—can move mountains.

"...Truly I tell you, if you have faith as small as a mustard seed, you can say to this mountain, 'Move from here to there,' and it will move. Nothing will be impossible for you."
—MATTHEW 17:20b

If a mustard-size grain of faith can move a mountain, do we need to spend time trying to get more faith, or do we just need to access the faith God has deposited in us? The truth is that we have exactly the measure of faith we need.

When we have difficulty seeing the Holy Spirit working in and through us, the problem does not stem from a lack of faith. *Who* moved the mountain in Matthew 20 and by what means? Was it moved by 'conjuring up' enough faith? Or did grace—the empowering presence of the Holy Spirit—move it on our behalf? The answer is that grace moved the mountain and faith played an important role. Faith was the ingredient that enabled us to keep our eyes fixed on God, waiting for Him to move the mountain that prevented us from moving forward. The waiting part is what enabled us to see the Holy Spirit at work on our behalf. Without faith, we would have taken a detour in an attempt to bypass the impediment on our own. The Holy Spirit does not have the opportunity to act when we move ahead of God instead of waiting on Him.

Matthew 17:20b reveals another important truth. If a mustard-size grain of faith can access enough grace to move a mountain, even the greatest of obstacles can be overcome. Limitations and barriers to doing God's work fall in the face of biblical faith. God's grace has no limits. It is sufficient in every situation.

"But he said to me, 'My grace is sufficient for you, for my power is made perfect in weakness.' Therefore I will boast all the more gladly about my weaknesses, so that Christ's power may rest on me." —II CORINTHIANS 12:9

As a new Christian, I experienced the sufficiency of God's grace when He presented the opportunity for me to share my faith with the computer repairpersons. I would like to say I continued moving uphill during the five years I worked for the company, but things went downhill the day Liz walked out the door.

My relationship with my boss was difficult and I was uncertain from one day to the next if I would be his favorite employee or his worst enemy. I prayed regularly for God to move me but when nothing happened, I decided to find a job on my own. I made contact with an electronics company that was excited about my credentials. After completing the interviewing process with one of the in-house recruiters, I was told I would be receiving three different offers from three different departments within the week. The next day I received a phone call from the recruiter informing me that every job requisition had been frozen and there would be no offers.

I remember the day so clearly. I fell to my knees and sobbed. My stomach hurt so much that I doubled over in pain. The hope of leaving my job and getting away from my boss had been quashed. I could not understand why God had closed the door for me to a new position.

My attitude improved when I stopped looking at my circumstances and fixed my eyes on God. The hope that had been lost was slowly renewed when I recalled the many ways God had worked in my life. He had always been faithful, and I recognized He had not deserted me. The problem was that I had attempted to 'move the mountain' on my own instead of waiting on Him.

Realizing the error of my ways, I confessed my sin to God and committed to remain at my present job for as long as He wanted me there. I was determined to put forth my best effort to serve and glorify God in spite of the difficult circumstances.

A few weeks later, I received a phone call from the executive manager of a technical school. The school was in need of a director for its electronics department and she had been given my name. The manager wanted to arrange an interview as soon as possible as the school was in a hurry to fill the position. I explained I was not in the market for a new job, but she refused to hang up until a meeting had been arranged.

I felt confused when I hung up the phone. Having made the decision to remain where I was and glorify God, I was reluctant to attend the interview. I quietly bowed my head and committed the process to God. I had already ventured out on my own, and I did not want to repeat my mistake.

God could not have made His will more apparent. Throughout the interview, the manager continually told me I was exactly the right person for the job. The school had been searching for someone with my qualifications for months, and the manager thought it was no accident she had been given my name. Toward the end of the interview, she told me the job was mine. A few details needed to be worked out, but I would be able to give my notice within the week.

The new job was amazing. My spirit soared when I recognized the Holy Spirit working in and through me to have an impact on the students and staff. The recognition I received in my new position was unprecedented for me. This was especially meaningful to me in light of my experience with my former supervisor. But there is more to the story.

One morning, about a year after I had been at the school, the Lord led me to Psalm 7:15 which says,

"Whoever digs a hole and scoops it out falls into the pit they have made."

"Lord," I asked, "what are You trying to tell me? Is someone digging a pit?"

My boss was waiting for me when I arrived at work. She announced that the owner of the company thought I was overloaded and could use an assistant. The candidate was already in the boss's office and I was to join them for the interview.

The Holy Spirit brought the Psalm to my mind and revealed the meaning while I was walking back to my office following the interview. The owner of the business was planning to throw me 'into the pit' by firing me.

I plopped down at my desk in disbelief, wondering how this could be happening. Everything had been going so well. Why was I going to be fired? My thoughts were interrupted when my boss called me to come to her office to discuss the candidate.

I felt speechless when I arrived at her office, but the Holy Spirit gave me exactly the right words: "I think the candidate is my replacement and I am going to be fired." My boss sat back in her chair in shock. "What makes you think that?" she asked. I told her about the Psalm the Lord had led me to that morning, and I explained that God had used the verse to reveal the truth of this situation. She was amazed and could not deny the truth of God's message. "Surely, you serve a living and true God," she said, "for you are going to be fired." My boss explained the owner of the company felt I had become too popular with the students and staff and he wanted me fired as soon as possible. He did not like competing for attention with a paid staff member.

There was no doubt in my mind God was totally in control of this situation. He had brought me to the school and it seemed apparent He was moving me. I just needed to wait on Him to direct my steps and reveal the work He had prepared for me.

Knowing this would come through prayer, I left for lunch and went to a nearby park to spend time with God.

I returned to work resting in the assurance God had a plan and purpose for me in this situation. He confirmed this as soon as I walked in the door. "Joanne," the receptionist said, "I have a message for you. The caller would not leave his phone number, but he said he would call you back. He told me I should give you his name and you would understand the purpose of the call."

I took the paper from the receptionist and smiled when I read it. The name on the paper was that of the recruiter I had been working with the prior year when all of the job requisitions at the electronics firm had been frozen.

I started my new job within a week. It, too, turned out to be an amazing opportunity. The position was truly a gift from God, and my new boss was wonderful. The greater gift was seeing the Holy Spirit work so clearly in my life, teaching me to walk by faith and experience His grace.

OUR FAITH NEEDS TO BE DEVELOPED

The problem with unmoved mountains (roadblocks) that prevent us from moving across the bridge rests in the fact that our faith is largely undeveloped. Much like the oil reserves that remained undeveloped because the experts could not figure out how to tap into them, undeveloped faith prevents us from 'tapping into' the fullness of God's grace. Undeveloped faith leads to our attempts to 'access the oil fields', drawing on our own strength rather than waiting on God.

Similar to many kingdom principles relating to our growth and development as children of the King, faith development is a process. We cannot develop faith on our own. It requires our participation, of course, but God is the Author and Developer of our faith. He primarily uses three different avenues to develop it: prayer, Bible study, and life's difficulties.

When God presents us with a particular assignment, it is never His intention that we complete it on our own. He wants to accomplish the work in and through us by grace through faith, but learning to operate by faith to access grace takes time. It does not happen overnight. We must become willing to break out of the cage and step onto the bridge. Then we must venture across, one step at a time. There are no shortcuts and there are no detours.

Figure 6 shows the interaction between faith, grace, and work. *By faith* we access grace. *Grace* accomplishes the work God gives us to do. When we experience the Holy Spirit working in and through us, our faith is developed.

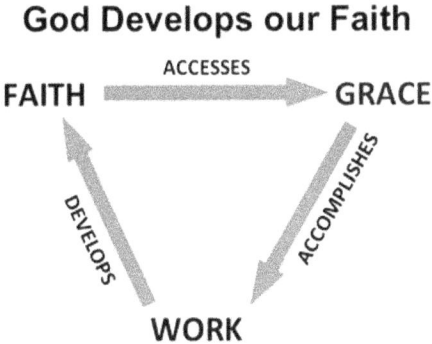

God Develops our Faith

FAITH ACCESSES → GRACE

DEVELOPS

ACCOMPLISHES

WORK

Figure 6

This process is repeated again and again throughout our lifetimes. When integrated with prayer and Bible study, our focus and confidence shift from the world economy to the kingdom economy.

Transitioning from the world economy to God's kingdom economy and learning to operate by grace and faith is rewarding. We experience the truth of God's Word as we see Him working in and through us in ways beyond our comprehension. We also experience challenges. Consider the Israelites when they departed Egypt and journeyed to the Promised Land. Drawing on their experiences can help us understand that we will experience trials along the way.

Learning to 'plug into' the power source, the Holy Spirit, is not as easy as it sounds. It takes time and it requires practice. At times, we will feel elated and fully charged, as though we are fully wired for electricity. There will also be times when we feel as though we are wired for electricity but all we can get to work is a kerosene lamp. But God is faithful. He will not forsake us. Over time, as we come to maturity in Him, we will discover that the rewards of crossing the bridge far outweigh the challenges.

CHAPTER SEVEN

Becoming a Person of Influence
A Growing Dependence on God

"...You were faithful with a few things, I will put you in charge of many things..." —MATTHEW 25:21b (NAS)

One of the first questions we usually ask when we meet someone is, "What do you do?" In the world economy the answer defines who we are. People assume we *are* what we *do*. In the secular economy there may not be a connection between *what* we do and *who* God created us to be. The link between work and purpose may be missing. In the kingdom economy, there is always a connection between our work and God's design for our lives. Kingdom living understands we are not defined by our vocation. We are *who* we are by God's design. Our work fits with His plans and purposes for our daily lives and eternity, but it does not define us.

Work in God's economy is represented as a series of concentric circles in figure 7. Each ring represents the different work assignments God reveals to us when we make our way across the bridge, learning to operate by grace, through faith. The entire sphere represents the lifetime of work God has prepared for us—kingdom work *He* wants to accomplish in and through us. Work inside these circles is an expression of *who* God created us to be; it provides us with the sense of significance for which we were created.

79

WORK IN GOD'S ECONOMY

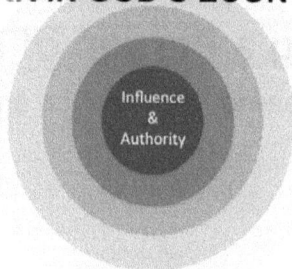

Figure 7

The small inner circle, labeled 'Influence & Authority', represents our starting point. It signifies the start of our new life in Christ. All of the work assignments God gives us as a new believer are located inside this small inner circle. He designed us to reign and rule inside our sphere. It is our place of dominion, our God-given area of influence and authority. When we are operating within our sphere by grace, we are of one mind with God, joined to Him in Spirit. Adam's life and work in the garden is an excellent example of this concept because he was given dominion over the entire garden. The garden, represented by the 'bull's-eye', was his sphere of influence. Each ring corresponds to the various work assignments God had prepared for him.

When we are operating within our sphere of influence and authority, it means the Holy Spirit reigns in our lives. It indicates we are operating by grace through faith, waiting on God to perform *His* work in and through us. When we wait on God, He draws people into our circle who have need of our service. The type of service inside our circle comes in many different forms.

It includes all of the work that is accomplished through the empowering presence of the Holy Spirit—paid and non-paid, religious and nonreligious—wherever God positions us. Work inside this circle is our God-given ministry. It is our act of spiritual worship.

The Holy Spirit uses many different ways to draw people into our sphere. An example of how He does this can be seen during the time Butch and I were at a copy center preparing workbooks for the Life Purpose Workshop. Butch was (and still is!) a hands-on person. He was gifted in efficiency and machinery; therefore, he immediately orchestrated the job at the copy center by organizing the materials and laying out the steps. He quickly had the process underway.

Butch was soon approached by a person experiencing problems with his copy machine. He needed Butch's help. Within minutes another person asked for Butch's help. Then another. And another. It was as though Butch had a sign on his forehead announcing his ability and availability.

No one approached me. Why? Because Butch was 'in his element' at the copy center, whereas I was not. People in need of Butch's expertise were drawn to him. Requesting his help came naturally to them.

SPHERE OF INFLUENCE AND AUTHORITY EXPANDED

Notice the size of the center circle in figure 8 has increased. Moving outward from the center, the circle has expanded into the next ring, indicating God has increased our sphere of influence and authority.

WORK IN GOD'S ECONOMY

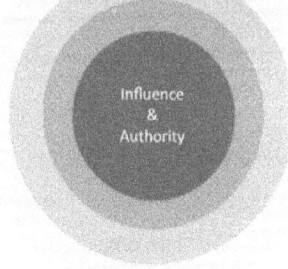

Influence
&
Authority

Figure 8

God is able to do this because grace and faith are at work in our lives. When *all* of the assignments inside the smaller inner circle are completed, it means God has developed enough of our faith to give us access to the grace we will need to operate in the next ring.

When God expands our sphere of influence and authority, He is saying, in essence, "Well done, my faithful servant." A 'well done' in the world economy assumes upward movement. It may mean we receive a pay increase or change in title, but promotion is not measured materially in the kingdom economy. God does not measure success with a monetary value or a job title. Though we have been trained to make that connection, living and working in God's economy requires a paradigm shift in our thinking. While there *may* be an increase in pay or a change in title when God increases our sphere of influence and authority, there could also be a decrease in salary or even a job loss.

A 'well done' for believers means we have proven ourselves to be faithful and that God entrusts us with greater responsibility.

"Whoever can be trusted with very little can also be trusted with much..." —LUKE 16:10a

Increased responsibility may look quite different for each of us, but the end result is that God is repositioning us. He is bringing us to the end of an assignment to position us for a new beginning.

An example of how God repositions us can be seen during the time I worked for the difficult boss at the electronics firm. The uncertainty of his mood swings caused me a great deal of anxiety. I prayed regularly for God to move me, but all of the job requisitions at the new company were frozen on the very day the offers were to have been extended. God had already prepared my next assignment, which would come through the recruiter, but the timing was off. I was not fully equipped, at that time, to handle the increased responsibility and authority that would come with the position. God protected me by preventing me from moving. When I finally gave up control and allowed God to direct my steps, He increased my sphere by repositioning me at the school. A year later God increased my sphere of influence and authority again when I learned I was going to be fired. Then the recruiter called.

SUCCESS REVISITED

There may be times when we are operating within our sphere of influence and authority that we feel as though God has abandoned us. I certainly felt that way when I worked at the electronics firm. But when we operate by grace, keeping our eyes fixed on God, we can serve Him and others with gladness, resting in the assurance He is in control. We need to recall the meaning of true success during those times when we experience doubt: *bringing glory to God on earth by completing the work He gives us to do.* We also need to remind ourselves that we are incapable of achieving true success on our own. It can only be realized through the empowering presence of the Holy Spirit.

There are many examples of true success throughout the Bible and history. We have no problem identifying some of those who have been successful. Billy Graham is a modern-day example. There can be no doubt that God increased Graham's sphere of influence over the years, exposing him to greater and greater numbers of people. But many examples of true success are not as apparent as Billy Graham's. When we 'go behind the scenes' to examine the lives of God's people, we see that success does not always mean smooth sailing.

Consider the disciple John, who was exiled to the island of Patmos. The world economy would have judged him a failure, but John's influence and scope of work increased dramatically when he was on the island. God used John's time there to pen the Revelation. His plan for John was that his sphere of influence and authority would reach all the way into the 21st century and beyond from the tiny island of Patmos.

Another example of a biblically successful individual is King David in the Old Testament. God promoted David from shepherding sheep to shepherding His flock. David's sphere of influence and authority was expanded from king of the field to king of a nation. Yet the world, in light of some of his early experiences hiding in caves and running from the malevolent pursuit of King Saul, would consider David to be a failure.

Hiding...running...unable to claim his rightful position. Is this the picture of success we want for ourselves? No. But in

David's situation, God used 'cave life' to develop his faith in preparation for kingship.

Joseph is an excellent Old Testament example of kingdom service. When Joseph was 17 years old, God gave him a glimpse of his future through a dream, which he boastfully shared with his brothers. His brothers' jealousy led them to sell Joseph to the Canaanites, and Joseph was carried away to Egypt.

God used the treachery of the brothers to expand Joseph's sphere of influence and authority by positioning him as the head of Potiphar's household. After being unjustly accused by Potiphar's wife and thrown into prison, God widened Joseph's sphere of influence and authority again by promoting him to chief steward of the prison. Joseph interpreted Pharaoh's dream at age 30 and he was promoted to the position of Vice Pharaoh, second in command only to Pharaoh himself.

Joseph's dependence on God increased through the years and God continued to broaden his assignments, setting the stage for Joseph's ultimate assignment at age 39—the preservation and rescue of the nation of Israel from certain death due to starvation.

Consider the breadth of experience Joseph needed to become Vice Pharaoh. Imagine the depth of knowledge it would require for him to administer the nationwide food program. In the world economy, he would need an MBA from the prestigious University of Egypt at the very least. In God's economy, Joseph earned his credentials through slavery and hard work. Each and every situation was used for Joseph's good and God's glory. As Joseph told his brothers:

"You intended to harm me, but God intended it for good to accomplish what is now being done, the saving of many lives"
—GENESIS 50:20

A visual representation of the highlights of Joseph's sphere of influence and authority are shown in figure 9.

LIFE'S LESSONS FROM JOSEPH

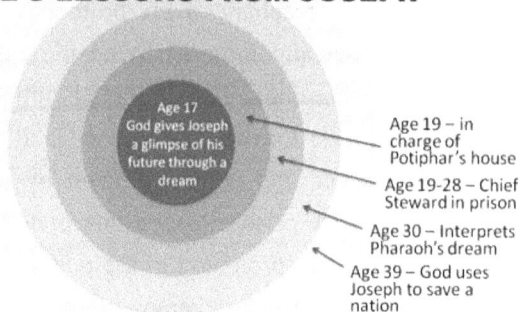

Age 17
God gives Joseph a glimpse of his future through a dream

Age 19 – in charge of Potiphar's house

Age 19-28 – Chief Steward in prison

Age 30 – Interprets Pharaoh's dream

Age 39 – God uses Joseph to save a nation

Figure 9

Certainly there was more to Joseph's life than is notated here. But in visualizing the highlights, we can see God used every aspect of Joseph's experiences to develop his faith and create a greater dependence on Him.

Jesus Christ provides us with the greatest example of the sphere of influence and authority. For three years his influence was primarily with the disciples. He was often criticized and ridiculed for His beliefs. Accused by the very ones He came to save, Jesus was sentenced to the cross. Yet, it was through the cross that His earthly sphere of   influence and authority was expanded beyond human comprehension. Much of the world judges Him a failure, an impostor, but from a kingdom perspective, Jesus is the most successful person the world has ever known. Kingdom thinking is radically opposite to the world's point of view.

When we finally get our minds and hearts around God's truths and allow the Holy Spirit to reign in our lives, we become better equipped to handle the difficulties that come our way. The only way we will ever experience the fullness of God's plans and purposes for our lives and find contentment in every situation is to step onto the bridge and embrace kingdom living.

A lifetime of kingdom living, content in our circumstances. How might that appear? As shown in figure 10, the center circle will have increased to its greatest capacity.

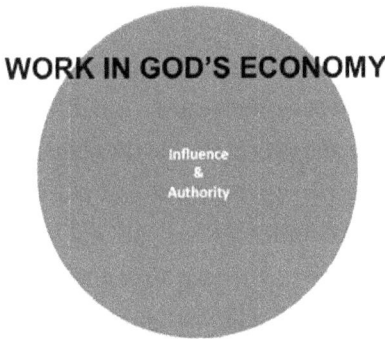

WORK IN GOD'S ECONOMY

Influence
&
Authority

Figure 10

This growth has occurred over a lifetime, one ring at a time. The person represented in this diagram has experienced true success—*bringing glory to God on earth by completing the work He gives us to do.* He has a lifetime of serving God and is familiar with bridge life. He has matured through a series of disappointments, difficulties, and achievements. He has full access to the grace in him. He has achieved congruency and experiences harmony in all areas of his life. He recognizes the hand of God in his daily life and work. He is assured that all of his work, regardless of where it takes place, is service to the King. Biblically speaking, this person experienced the fullness of Adam's garden life on earth.

A look at historical characters in the Bible reveals this person could be almost anyone—Abraham, Moses, Ruth, David, Esther, Paul, Peter, Dorcas, Mary Magdalene, or Lydia. The Bible speaks of many people who exercised their faith to experience grace. Yet none were more important than you or me. None had more to offer God than you or me. They simply understood they were nothing without God. None had ever heard of the sphere of influence and authority, but they lived it on a daily basis.

God never wastes time or opportunities. He gives us precisely the experiences we need to fulfill His purpose for our lives and complete the work He has prepared for us. God uses life's trials to bring personal growth and maturity. When we are in the midst of difficulties or we are not moving forward as quickly as we might like, we need to remind ourselves God is in control. He is maturing us and preparing us for our future assignments by strengthening our spiritual connection through prayer, His Word, and life's challenges.

The paradigm through which we view success in the world economy is not consistent with kingdom living. Worldly thinking left unchecked draws us away from God's grace. Satan is a master at rendering us ineffective. He plans strategies and presents opportunities to draw us away from the work God has prepared for us. When we accept work that does not align with our God-given design, we remove ourselves from our God-given sphere of influence and authority and limit ourselves from experiencing biblical success.

Our God-given gifts and strengths frequently work against us in the world economy. Promotion may actually decrease our sphere of influence and authority by giving us responsibility that is outside our gifted area. Promotion in God's economy increases our sphere of influence and authority by giving us greater responsibility within our gifted area.

If we are to succeed biblically, we need to continually remind ourselves the kingdom economy is completely opposite to the secular world economy. We need to evaluate every opportunity in light of our gifting and trust the Holy Spirit will nudge us to move in the right direction. We have been well-trained in the ways of the world to believe we are defined by *what* we do. Our significance is characterized by the size of a paycheck or a job title and, to a large degree, by having a paid job outside the home. In God's economy, our purpose can be fully satisfied wherever God places us. What enlightenment for all believers!

There is another kingdom economy success story from Butch's life. Butch was supervising an extensive home remodel which required the landscaping to be removed, bringing the yard down to bare dirt. Knowing that the Arizona desert is dusty, Butch watered the client's backyard every day to keep the dust down. Doing this was something that came naturally to Butch. He did not have to think about doing it or see the need to discuss it with anybody, he just did it.

Unbeknownst to Butch, the client's neighbor was watching the progress on the house. She also watched him water the dirt.

When Butch left the job site each day, the neighbor and the client would get together to discuss the progress that had been made on the home. They would also discuss Butch's 'odd behavior' with regard to watering the dirt. Neither had ever seen a contractor care enough to go that extra mile. While they understood the purpose of Butch's doing it and they were most appreciative, they were surprised that he would go to such extremes to keep the jobsite clean.

On the final day of the project, the client and the neighbor approached Butch, wanting to know if he was a Christian. They explained they had come to this conclusion because he had been watering the dirt. They knew very little about Christianity but felt certain only a Christian would care so much about the client and the neighbors to water the dirt.

Watering dirt was significant in God's kingdom economy. It was Butch's spiritual act of worship.

CHAPTER EIGHT

Paradise Restored

Our Final Destination

*"Brethren, I do not regard myself as having laid hold of it yet;
but one thing I do: forgetting what lies behind and reaching
forward to what lies ahead, I press on toward the goal for the
prize of the upward call of God in Christ Jesus."*
—PHILIPPIANS 3:13–14 (NAS)

Return with me to God's eternal workroom where we observed God the Father, Jesus Christ the Son, the Holy Spirit, and the angelic beings fulfilling their individual work assignments. We witnessed Adam contentedly living and working on the earth, designed by the Creator to participate in the garden work surrounding him. Created to reign and rule over the physical earth, Adam played a vital role in God's eternal plans and purposes.

Now the drama shifts from past events and present living to our sure and coming future. Imagine crossing the threshold into eternity to arrive at your final destination—the new earth. Streets of gold glisten before you. Your Savior takes your hand and welcomes you into God's eternal kingdom.

You are fully aware of your surroundings. You experience a sense of familiarity, yet nothing is the same as it was on earth. Your memory is sharper than it has ever been. Your personality, thoughts, intellect, gifts, and abilities have been perfected. You are surrounded by His Bride, the Church, clothed in splendor. Is that your earthly mother over there, your sister, brother, husband, best friend? You look around and see the people Hebrews 11-12 refers to as the "cloud of witnesses" who arrived before you. Intuitively, you recognize them all. Your heart overflows with love for God. You are filled with a desire to bow down and worship Him.

You wish you could remain forever, but your unfinished work beckons you back to the bridge. You return to earth, more determined than ever to operate by grace to complete the work God has prepared for you.

Following God's plans and purposes for us on earth and living in His kingdom economy are wonderful, but life in the eternal realm, where we are in the presence of Jesus Christ, our Lord and Savior, is far superior. Paul understood this. Philippians 1:2 states:

"For to me, to live is Christ and to die is gain."

What exactly did Paul know? What was the gain he foresaw?

The Bible speaks of the time when God will destroy this earth and all of its works and create a brand new earth. The garden will be restored and the saved will dwell in righteousness forever. God reveals this magnificent truth in His Word:

"For behold, I create new heavens and a new earth..."
— ISAIAH 65:17a (NKJV)

" 'For as the new heavens and the new earth which I will make, shall remain before Me,' says the LORD, 'so shall your descendants and your name remain.' " —ISAIAH 66:22 (NKJV)

"Nevertheless we, according to His promise, look for new heavens and a new earth in which righteousness dwells."

—II PETER 3:13 (NKJV)

"Now I saw a new heaven and a new earth, for the first heaven and the first earth had passed away. Also there was no more sea. Then I, John, saw the holy city, New Jerusalem, coming down out of heaven from God, prepared as a bride adorned for her husband." —REVELATION 21:1–2 (NKJV)

The new earth is a real place, seated in the eternal realm. As believers in Jesus Christ, this is our final destination. We will live forever in the new earth, reigning and ruling with Christ in our glorified bodies. We are members of a royal priesthood, granted full citizenship in the kingdom. This is why Christ died for us—to restore us to the position God originally intended for mankind. This is why Jesus gave up His place in the heavenly realm and entered into a physical body forever.

We will be living and working in a grace-based economy in the new earth, without hindrance of sin. There will no longer be any curse. We will each fulfill our rightful positions, using our God-given gifts and talents to serve and glorify Christ and to contribute to the care of the earth. This is our sure and coming future:

"Then the angel showed me the river of the water of life, as clear as crystal, flowing from the throne of God and of the Lamb down the middle of the great street of the city. On each side of the river stood the tree of life, bearing twelve crops of fruit, yielding its fruit every month. And the leaves of the tree are for the healing of the nations. No longer will there be any curse. The throne of God

and of the Lamb will be in the city, and his servants will serve him. They will see his face, and his name will be on their foreheads. There will be no more night. They will not need the light of a lamp or the light of the sun, for the Lord God will give them light. And they will reign forever and ever."

—REVELATION 22:1–5

"And I heard a loud voice from heaven saying, 'Behold, the tabernacle of God is with men, and He will dwell with them, and they shall be His people. God Himself will be with them and be their God.'... These words are true and faithful."

—REVELATION 21:3; 5 (NKJV)

The enjoyments and comforts of life in the new earth will be unlike anything we have ever experienced. In the world economy, we experience uncertainty and our lives are often overshadowed by the 'what-ifs'. The new earth will be utterly different. There will be no uncertainty, no regrets. The brief applause we experience for our good work on this earth will fade in comparison to the rich blessings we will receive in the new earth.

That we will be serving Christ and reigning with Him assures us that our work in the new earth will be perfect. Our never-ending experience will be one of fellowship, joy in the Lord, and intimacy with God. Work will naturally be service to God—our spiritual act of worship. He will meet all of our needs, and we will freely eat from the fruit of the tree of life.

Every aspect of our being will be alive to God in the new earth—body, soul, and spirit. This is not just a spiritual experience. We will be 'totally there'. We will live there physically, relationally, and spiritually. If you pinch yourself, you will feel it.

What might this be like? Think of the most elegant master-planned community you have ever seen. Beautifully crafted homes set back from quiet streets. Huge shade trees lining the sidewalks. Bountiful flower gardens with mounds of color. Perfectly manicured lawns. Lavish shrubs and bushes. Fluffy clouds drifting lazily through a blue sky. Breezes rustling through the leaves. Everything you need and desire within walking distance.

You can see yourself walking along the lusciously landscaped paths winding along ponds. You can feel the cool breeze blowing through your hair. You take a deep breath. Ahh! The aroma of freshly mown lawns and the varying scents of the flowers waft through the air. And you wonder what life would be like here.

Now, realize this master-planned community is, at best, a cheap imitation of what is yet to come. Ours will be a community planned by the True Master's hands. The plans had already been drawn before Jesus told the disciples that He was going to prepare a place for them. (John 14:2 —NKJV)

OUR WORK HAS ETERNAL IMPORTANCE

God does not want us to remain ignorant of His truths. He wants us to live informed lives that reflect a growing understanding and application of His Word. He wants us to know that how we live today shapes our eternity.

The eternally important question is: Who will power my work—the Holy Spirit or the flesh? Asking Christ into our lives guarantees our citizenship in the kingdom, but our residency on earth impacts our eternal position. Where we choose to live and work during our tenure on earth—in the secular world economy or God's kingdom economy—has undeniable eternal importance. Our work will never earn salvation. That is not the purpose of work. Salvation is by grace through faith alone. Once we accept Jesus as our Savior, our works are the evidence of our faith. True faith produces godly works. This is why James tells us faith without works is dead:

"What use is it, my brethren, if someone says he has faith but he has no works? Can that faith save him?... Even so faith, if it has no works, is dead, being by itself. But someone may well say, 'You have faith and I have works; show me your faith without the works, and I will show you my faith by my works.'... But are you willing to recognize, you foolish fellow, that faith without works is useless? Was not Abraham our father justified by works when he offered up Isaac his son on the altar? You see that faith was working with his works, and as a result of the works, faith was perfected. ... You see that a man is justified by works and not by faith alone. ... For just as the body without the spirit is dead, so also faith without works is dead."
—JAMES 2:14, 17–18, 20–23, 26 (NAS)

OUR WORK FOLLOWS US INTO ETERNITY

Our work is significant to God. So significant, in fact, that it follows us into eternity:

"Then I heard a voice from heaven saying to me, 'Write: Blessed are the dead who die in the Lord from now on.'" "'Yes,' says the Spirit, 'that they may rest from their labors, and their works follow them.'" —REVELATION 14:13 (NKJV)

"Resting from their labors" is specific to believers who are martyred during the great tribulation; however, all work—the work of believers and nonbelievers from every time period on earth—follows them into eternity.

While we are unable to know the specifics of our work following us into eternity, we can say with certainty that all of the good works God produces in and through us have lasting value.

"I know that everything God does will remain forever..."

—ECCLESIASTES 3:14a (NAS*)*

Throughout the years that Butch and I taught the Life Purpose Workshop, I met with participants one-on-one to help bring clarity to their God-given gift. During a two-week period when I had been asking God for greater understanding of how our works follow us into eternity, every person with whom I met had been endowed with the gift of music. This unusual situation led me to conclude that God wanted to reveal something to me.

A young man, after learning that God had given him the gift of music, was deeply saddened. He had even written three songs and produced a demo tape, but he saw no way of ever being able to support himself through music. His present position as a seminary recruiter was unfulfilling, but it was a source of income and he was reluctant to make a change.

My heart went out to him. Clearly, he had been given the gift of music and I wanted to encourage him. Suddenly a thought came to me. I grabbed pencil and paper and wrote: "I want to encourage you to write the songs God has put in your heart today, for the songs you are writing on earth will be sung in eternity."

Take a moment to consider this revelation. Close your eyes and visualize life in the new earth. Imagine yourself walking on streets of gold with the choir singing the *Hallelujah Chorus.* Envision the presence of other earthly works, possibly accomplished by grace: Michelangelo's statue of David. Da Vinci's painting of the Mona Lisa or the Last Supper. John Bunyan's book, *The Pilgrim's Progress,* Martin Luther's *95 Theses.* The possibilities are endless. Work on earth hat is inspired and directed by the Holy Spirit remains forever.

OUR WORK IS JUDGED IN ETERNITY

The Bible reveals God will judge our work in eternity. This coming judgment is completely different from the judgment of sin, which has already occurred.

"For God will bring every work into judgment, including every secret thing, Whether good or evil."

—ECCLESIASTES 12:14 (NKJV)

"And if you call on the Father, who without partiality judges according to each one's work, conduct yourselves throughout the time of your stay here in fear..." —I PETER 1:17 (NKJV)

"Also to You, O Lord, belongs mercy; for You render to each one according to his work." —PSALM 62:12 (NKJV)

When we meet the Lord face-to-face and our work is laid out before Him, one of two things will occur: we will be rewarded, or we will suffer loss. Grace-based work brings rewards, whereas self-driven work is destined to be burned. We are saved through our relationship with Jesus Christ, but the work we accomplished apart from God will prove to be an utter loss. This is revealed in I Corinthians 3:9–15 (NKJV):

"For we are God's fellow workers; you are God's field, you are God's building. According to the grace of God which was given to me, as a wise master builder I have laid the foundation, and another builds on it. But let each one take heed how he builds on it. For no other foundation can anyone lay than that which is laid, which is Jesus Christ. Now if anyone builds on this foundation with gold, silver, precious stones, wood, hay, straw, each one's work will become clear; for the Day will declare it, because it will be revealed by fire; and the fire will test each one's work, of what sort it is. If anyone's work which he has built on it endures, he will receive a reward. If anyone's work is burned, he will suffer loss; but he himself will be saved, yet so as through fire."

WORK WITHOUT FAITH HAS NO ETERNAL VALUE

The truth of God's Word brings us great comfort. It is a relief to know we will not stand before the Lord in eternity giving an accounting of our sin. But knowing God will examine and pronounce judgment on our works in eternity may be cause for alarm.

If faith without work is dead, then the opposite is also true: work without faith is also dead. Faithless works may appear good in that they contribute to the well-being of others, but they have no eternal value. Work without faith, regardless of where it is performed, is made of straw. It is destined for the fire.

This should stop us in our tracks, particularly when we glance behind to see what is following us and picture ourselves standing before Christ with our work spread out for Him to

99

examine! Your work...my work...some accomplished by grace...
others through our own strength. Church work without eternal value.
Missionary work with no eternal significance. Sacrificial work in a
corporation done only for the sake of a paycheck. Homemaking done
grudgingly, without faith.

THE REWARD FOR WORK

Return with me to the new earth. Center stage is Jesus
Christ, surrounded by His Bride, the Church, and other believers,
contentedly working in harmony to glorify the King and care for
God's creation. *Stop!* Don't take a seat. You are no longer a
spectator. You are a royal participant.

Designed by God to participate in His eternal plans and
purposes for eternity, you are secure in your environment and
intimacy with God. You receive your work assignments directly
from the King. Variety and challenge characterize your
responsibilities. You are filled with purpose as you set out each
morning to complete your assignments, anticipating another
great day. Everything you do is meaningful and ultimately a gift
of service to your Creator. Life and work are one fantastic
worship service.

You end each day with a great sense of satisfaction and
fulfillment. Looking back at what was accomplished, you know
in your heart that your work is good...really good. It is your best.

Why would God assign mankind work in the new earth? As
with God's debut of Adam in the garden, work is an underlying
principle best understood in light of whom the Creator is—a
working God. If the Godhead's work never ceases, neither does
man's.

God's plan for mankind was that he would reign and rule
with Him forever, living and working in the earth:

"...rule over the fish of the sea and over the birds of the sky and over every living thing that moves on the earth."

—GENESIS1:28b (NAS)

Adam's sin distanced man from God, but it did not change God's overarching plans and purposes for mankind. His redemptive plan to restore what had been lost through the Fall was already in place before the foundation of the world. The new earth had already been framed in the heavens before the Fall took place. God gave John a glimpse of our future estate from the Island of Patmos (reference Revelation 22:1–5).

These verses leave no room for doubt. Believers will reign with Jesus Christ in the new earth forever and ever. To 'reign' is to have a position of authority, to be in a place of service that yields influence. In the new earth, we will all have a place of service. We will be assigned work that is deeply satisfying and fits exactly with our God-given gifts and talents, but we will not all have the same position.

In the new earth, we will be rewarded for our earthly work that survives the test of the fire. (I Corinthians 3:9-15) What, exactly, is the reward? A biblical study of work leads to the conclusion the reward is increased authority and greater responsibility.

What we do on this earth profoundly impacts our eternal position. As believers, we are writing our resumes for eternity. The words of evangelist Reinhard Bonnke emphasize that a successful resume is a faith-based resume: *"When you do business with people, you need money. When you do business with God, you need faith. Faith is the currency of the Kingdom of God."* Without faith, we will never experience true biblical success. Faith is the mark of a successful resume.

ETERNAL FATE OF WORK: THE HEART OF THE MATTER

God does not look at outward appearances. He looks straight to the heart of the matter. His criterion is simple: Who accomplished the work? The Holy Spirit or you? Grace-based work does not give us freedom to do less than our best, but it places responsibility for the outcome squarely where it belongs: in God's hands.

What falls into the realm of grace-based work? Looks can be deceiving. When viewed through our 'earth eyes', we are unable to discern which works have eternal value and which do not. All work—religious and nonreligious—can be of the world or of the kingdom. But the question is always the same: Is your work faith-based, directed by the Holy Spirit, or are you setting out on your own, relying on your perceived strengths, forgetting about the gift of the Holy Spirit in you?

When the Holy Spirit is working in and through us, our work is always of the kingdom, regardless of where it takes place. Conversely, if the work is being done through ourselves, void of the Holy Spirit, our work is secular. Secular work includes everything we do on our own, in any setting. *Where* we accomplish the work is not the determining factor. Church work does not fall into the kingdom category unless it is grace-based. Missionary work does not have kingdom value unless it is Spirit-driven. Teaching in a public school can be of the kingdom, but not if it is self-driven. The work of a politician can have eternal value, but not if it is accomplished through the flesh.

As believers, it is important to examine our daily activities. It is far too easy to deceive ourselves into thinking we are doing God's work when in fact, we are acting on our own. If we truly want to serve God, our responsibility is to study the Word, immerse ourselves in prayer, and make ourselves available to Him. We must become willing to go where He calls us to go and do what He calls us to do. We need to evaluate our motives every day.

"Examine yourselves as to whether you are in the faith. Test yourselves. Do you not know yourselves, that Jesus Christ is in you?" —II CORINTHIANS13:5 (NKJV)

God's truths have the capacity to transform our lives if we act on them. In all likelihood, we will all suffer some degree of loss when we meet Christ, but as we mature in Him, we become the person God created us to be. When we experience the Spirit working in and through us, we know that grace is never in vain.

"But by the grace of God I am what I am, and His grace toward me was not in vain; but I labored more abundantly than they all, yet not I, but the grace of God which was with me."

—I CORINTHIANS 15:10 (NKJV)

CHAPTER NINE

Biblical Gifts

Unwrapping the Mystery of Biblical Gifts

"...but through love serve one another."
—GALATIANS 5:13c (NAS)

Once we understand work as God intends it, we can step onto the bridge toward the kingdom economy. As we make our way across, we must dig deeper into God's Word to understand how He has uniquely designed each one of us for work.

I vividly remember reading the announcement in my church bulletin years ago inviting people to attend a spiritual gift class. Believing it would benefit me in my quest to learn more about God's Word, particularly in the area of work, I signed up that day.

At the first class, we completed a spiritual gift inventory. The instructor explained spiritual gifts were special 'graces' from God to be used for the edification of believers. We were then given a list of activities consistent with our spiritual gift. We were encouraged to choose our ideal area of 'ministry service' from the list and volunteer at the church for a few hours each week.

I thought about the class over the following weeks and months and realized something did not seem right to me. With my belief that God has uniquely gifted each person for work and that we are to pursue our God-given calling, I was determined to dig deeper into the Bible to learn more about biblical gifts.

My beliefs regarding spiritual gifts were challenged as I continued to study God's Word. I concluded there are three types of gifts presented in the Bible: office, spiritual, and functional. Each is unique and given for a different purpose; however, they are easily confused. For example, there is an office gift of Teacher and a functional gift of Teacher, yet they are not the same gift. The office gift of Teacher is a position, whereas the functional gift of Teacher is a passion. Not all persons with the functional gift of Teacher are called into the office position of Teacher.

Office gifts enable believers to function within a specific office of leadership in the corporate Body (the Church) for the purpose of directing the members. Not everyone has an office gift. Office gifts are listed in Ephesians 4:11-12 (NAS) and they do not change.

"And He gave some as apostles, and some as prophets, and some as evangelists, and some as pastors and teachers, for the equipping of the saints for the work of service, to the building up of the body of Christ..."

Spiritual gifts are the manifestation or supernatural demonstration of the Holy Spirit working in a believer for the common good of the Body. Unlike office gifts, they are not permanent. They come and go at the discretion of the Holy Spirit, operating at different times through believers to glorify God and encourage the Body. Spiritual gifts can change; office gifts and functional gifts do not change. In fact, it is possible to experience a spiritual gift one time and never experience it again. The Holy Spirit is not limited by our humanness. He is able to manifest Himself in different ways at different times, at His choosing.

An example of a spiritual gift can be seen on the day of Pentecost when the Holy Spirit rested upon the disciples and gave them the supernatural ability to speak in other languages.

"When the day of Pentecost had come, they were all together in one place. And suddenly there came from heaven a noise like a violent rushing wind, and it filled the whole house where they were sitting. And there appeared to them tongues as of fire distributing themselves, and they rested on each one of them. And they were all filled with the Holy Spirit and began to speak with other tongues, as the Spirit was giving them utterance." —ACTS 2:1–4 (NAS)

Spiritual gifts are listed in I Corinthians 12:1, 7–11 (NAS):

"Now concerning spiritual gifts, brethren, I do not want you to be unaware...But to each one is given the manifestation of the Spirit for the common good. For to one is given the word of wisdom through the Spirit, and to another the word of knowledge according to the same Spirit; to another faith by the same Spirit, and to another gifts of healing by the one Spirit, and to another the effecting of miracles, and to another prophecy, and to another the distinguishing of spirits, to another various kinds of tongues, and to another the interpretation of tongues. But one and the same Spirit works all these things, distributing to each one individually just as He wills."

Spiritual gifts do not pertain to our place of service. They cannot be used to determine our life's purpose. To discern how

God designed us to serve and to discover our passion in life, we need to identify our functional gift.

Functional gifts are key to understanding the function for which we are created. They help us discover God's purpose for our lives and identify the work He has prepared for us. Functional gifts provide the framework for the way we think, feel, make decisions, and relate to others.

If we were tools, discovering our functional gift would tell us if we are a paintbrush, saw, hammer or another type of tool. This would establish the type of service for which we were created. If we were a paintbrush, we would paint. If a saw, we would do the work of a saw.

The problem with this illustration is that we are not tools. We are human beings designed for relationship. Yet the example of tools helps us understand the significance of functional gifts. It helps us discover how God designed us to perform certain functions and how our function is consistent with the work He has prepared for us.

When we put ourselves into the Creator's hands, we see Him work through us in ways that fit with our design wherever we are needed. When we work with God in accordance with our design, we are in full-time ministry and we experience true success: *bringing glory to God on earth by completing the work He gives us to do.*

Functional gifts are also referred to as motivational or redemptive gifts. These are the gifts that motivate us to action and they are redeemed at the moment of our conversion. Every aspect of our being was redeemed when Christ died on the cross—our mind, heart, body, soul, thoughts, relationships, work, and functional gift. We are being renewed and transformed daily through Christ.

Functional gifts are directly linked to the work God prepared in advance for us. They are permanent and though they can be developed, they do not change.

There are seven functional gifts: prophecy, serving, teaching, exhortation, giving, leading, and showing mercy.

"Since we have gifts that differ according to the grace given to us, each of us is to exercise them accordingly: if prophecy, according to the proportion of his faith; if service, in his serving; or he who teaches, in his teaching; or he who exhorts, in his exhortation; he who gives, with liberality; he who leads, with diligence; he who shows mercy, with cheerfulness." —ROMANS 12:6–8 (NAS)

While there are only seven functional gifts, each of us is unique as no two people have the same personality, thoughts, interactions, feelings, capacities, and so on. God endowed each one of us when He shaped and formed us in the womb with many different gifts and capacities. He gave each of us a 'portion' of each of the seven functional gifts, but we have *one* primary functional gift.

Our primary functional gift does not represent the totality of our design. It is the 'umbrella' under which all of our other gifts and capacities are clustered. Therefore, it is important that we identify and embrace our *primary* functional gift. Doing so provides us with a starting point for fulfilling God's purpose for us. At the same time, we will spend our lives discovering the other aspects of our makeup that contribute to our uniqueness.

It is similar to the example of tools. Paintbrushes, saws, and hammers represent the various umbrellas of tools but each umbrella shelters a cluster of more than one tool. The tools under one umbrella serve the same basic purpose, but each has a unique use. There are different ranges and capacities to their design. For example, if I were painting a wall I might choose a large brush, a roller, or a spray gun. If I were painting a paint-by-number picture, I would choose a small brush or perhaps even four or five different-sized brushes. This is the way it is with functional gifts.

Discovering our primary functional gift reveals the 'umbrella' under which we each belong, but it is not until we discern our underlying gifts that we begin to grasp the unique range and capacity of our design. This occurs over time as we study God's Word, spend time in prayer, avail ourselves to Him, and learn to operate by grace and faith. When we are faithful to complete the work God has prepared for us and He expands our sphere of influence and authority, He improves our vision and gives us a greater understanding of His plans and purposes for us. He also gives us additional insights into our gifting.

The fact that we are all unique and there are different ranges and capacities to our designs is not an indicator that we lack something. We have 100% of everything we need to complete the work God gives us and we lack nothing. Our goal is to identify and embrace our *primary* functional gift and trust God to develop it. We need to remind ourselves, daily, that we are writing our resumes for eternity. The gifts we are using on earth are the same gifts we will be using in the new earth. We will be rewarded in eternity for our stewardship on this earth. Those who are faithful stewards here will receive greater opportunities for service in the new earth.

With this understanding of biblical gifts, let's look at the characteristics of the seven functional gifts. Functional gifts can help identity our area of passion, but they are not a position. As we look at each different gift, be aware that the functional gifts in Romans 12:6–8 (NAS) are not the same as the office gifts in Ephesians 4:11 (NAS) or the spiritual gifts in I Corinthians 12:1, 7–11 (NAS), even though they have similar names. I also want to caution you that any gift assessments or inventories you have completed in the past may not be applicable to the functional gifts described in this book. As you read through each of the descriptions, ask God to reveal the primary functional gift He has given you.

THE PROPHET

Prophets can be described as Logicians, Theorists, or Philosophers. They are relentless problem solvers, created by God to conduct research. They improve the quality of our world and contribute to our lives by solving the problems the rest of us are unable to solve. One of the Prophet's greatest strengths is the ability to combine biblical truths to come up with concepts and principles God put in motion to govern the universe and our lives. The Prophet draws on these concepts and rearranges them to apply to a multitude of situations. Something a Prophet might say is: "Oh, I can do that," or, "If you do that, this will happen," or, "It's the principle of the thing."

I have the functional gift of Prophet. When Butch died from cancer, all I could do for months was to sit in a chair and weep. If you have experienced the death of someone you love, particularly a spouse, you understand how I felt. God spent almost fifteen years knitting us together in marriage to become one and then suddenly Butch was gone. I felt as though half of me had been torn away and I could not understand why God had allowed Butch to die.

Well-meaning friends would call and quote scripture to me. They would encourage me to read the Bible or tell me that I needed to go to church. I was not able to do any of those things because I was so devastated. I believed the Word, but I needed something more personal than a Bible verse or a sermon.

God knew that. He met me right there in my living room as I sat weeping in my chair. In His knowledge of my design and His love for me, God met my need. He revealed Himself to me through the principles that He set in motion to govern our lives and universe—the law of faith; the law of sin and death; the principle of cause and effect; the principle of healing, sickness, and disease. God saw me through these concepts and eventually brought me to a place of acceptance. This is typical of the way God reveals Himself to Prophets and helps them solve problems.

Prophets are people of vision. They see beyond the obvious and they have an understanding of cause and effect. Prophets are attuned to the universal laws of nature and they understand the consequences when these universal laws are violated. The depth of their understanding gives Prophets the ability to predict problems that will occur if God's laws are violated. For example, based on the Prophet's knowledge of the universal laws and principles that bring balance to the environment, a Prophet will recognize the consequences of disturbing the ozone layer.

Prophets thrive on and embrace change. They seek to improve or change things when they run out of problems to solve. In the workplace, the Prophet would rather quit than be stuck with the status quo. They see in terms of black and white. There is no gray in their world.

Those who do not have this gift may have a hard time understanding and appreciating Prophets, but without them our own understanding would be limited. We would live in a world without principles and without vision. We would lack answers to many of the problems we face daily.

THE SERVER

Servers can be described as Doers, Supporters, or Maintainers. They are designed to meet the immediate practical and physical needs of others. Servers are the caretakers of the world. They see the good in others and desire to offer their personal support and practical service to free others to do what they do best.

Servers are results-oriented people with a preference for short-term projects in which they can produce a visible result or achieve an objective. They lose interest if the project drags on too long or the scope of the work keeps changing. These are hands-on people, designed for efficiency. They enjoy freedom of movement and may have a preference for the outdoors.

Servers are most effective when they have clarity of task, understand their role, and are permitted to function independently to complete the job at hand. They prefer to know exactly what is expected to avoid 'second guessing'. A common expression for a Server is, "Just do it."

The type of service they provide is critical. They are down-to-earth people who keep both feet solidly on the ground. They are steadfast and reliable and can be counted on to do a job well. Servers are vital to improving the quality of our daily lives. Like doctors and nurses in the operating room, they willingly serve in difficult environments or circumstances of life.

Those who do not have the functional gift of Server frequently underrate this gift. To fully appreciate and embrace the Server's value and contribution, we need only consider what life would be like without them. If there were no Servers, there would be no one to meet our physical and practical needs—no bankers, automotive repair persons, grocery store clerks, restaurant cooks, food servers, taxi drivers, and flight attendants. Without Servers, we would be limited from achieving the potential God has placed in us because our time would be consumed trying to care for ourselves and meet our own physical and practical needs.

Steve, whose functional gift is Server, worked as a fraud investigator in a bank. His customers were interested in profit and loss. However, Steve was not. Though he could perform the functions that were required to do his job, as many of us can, he struggled in his relationships with his coworkers and clients because wanting to make a profit was unnatural to him. At the end of the day, profits were the furthest thing from Steve's mind.

Steve had a lifelong interest in the arts. He thought about becoming an artist in high school but chose a different direction when he was told how difficult it would be to earn a living in the arts. In his free time, he attended ballets, concerts, and theatrical productions. After work, he often stopped to listen to music while his coworkers gathered at the local bar for a beer. This caused Steve to realize that he related to artistic, creative people rather than those with whom he worked.

Over time, as Steve prayed and sought God's clarity for his work situation, the Lord opened doors for him so that he could develop relationships with some of the artists he had met throughout the years. When these relationships deepened, the Holy Spirit provided an opportunity for Steve to begin working in a box office, selling CDs and books at concerts, and ushering guests to their seats. Not only did serving the artists bring Steve a great deal of satisfaction and hope for his future, but it also encouraged him to pray that God would expand his sphere of influence and authority by bringing more creative, artistic people into his life.

THE TEACHER

Teachers communicate truth and information to equip and enlighten others. They are designed to come alongside the rest of us to help us grow and mature. Teachers may also be called Learners, Validators, Evaluators, or Information Gatherers.

The functional gift of Teacher is not a position. Teachers are much more interested in conducting research and writing textbooks than presenting the material. If asked to present the information, they may agree to do so, but they would be most comfortable one-on-one or in small group situations. In a classroom setting, they would lean toward factual courses such as science, chemistry, or health.

Teachers are motivated to learn. They have a preference for conducting research, evaluating information, and documenting results. When presented with new information, Teachers are slow to accept it. They need time to digest it and cannot be rushed into drawing a conclusion. For this reason, Teachers tend to discount personal experience. If the facts are not aligned from their perspective, the information is probably not true. Before Teachers will believe something, they need to see proof. These are the people that believe the "the proof is in the pudding." Something a Teacher might say is, "Prove it" or, "Where does it say that?"

It is easy to confuse the functional gift of Teacher with the functional gift of Prophet. This is because both gifts deal with information and research; however, the major difference is that the Teacher takes information at face value, whereas the Prophet goes deeper to extrapolate concepts and apply principles to a variety of situations. The Teacher would never do this.

For example, if a Teacher were asked if he is proficient at word-processing systems, he would stick to the facts and name the specific program on which he is experienced. The Prophet would announce that he could use any word-processing system, even though his actual experience may have been limited to only one or two systems. The Prophet does this because he understands the underlying design concepts for word processing systems. The Prophet might even go so far as to boldly state that he could become proficient with any word-processing system in only a few hours. The Teacher would never declare this and he might even think the Prophet is being dishonest.

Teachers are prolific readers and writers. Examples of something they might write include instruction manuals, travel guides, commentaries, encyclopedias, dictionaries, or textbooks. If there were no Teachers, we would live in an information void. There would be no one to enlighten us, equip us, provide instruction, or nurture our minds to intellectually grow.

When Butch and I taught the Life Purpose Workshop, the Teachers were always the last ones to accept the truth of the material. They questioned what was being presented and wanted a specific verse to prove every point. But by the end of the workshop, after having heard the full presentation based on the truth of God's Word, they no longer doubted the validity of the teaching.

THE EXHORTER

Exhorters are designed to influence the actions, attitudes, and behaviors of others. They recognize the potential for growth in people. Instead of seeing obstacles or roadblocks, Exhorters see the path forward. Something an Exhorter might say is, "This is an opportunity for growth."

Exhorters can be described as Motivators, Persuaders, Communicators, or Encouragers. They inspire others to learn. They are able to take the information a Teacher writes and present it in a way that motivates others to learn it. Exhorters integrate stories and share personal experiences to make the presentation more exciting and help listeners grasp the information being presented. A person with the functional gift of Teacher would not take this same approach. The Teacher's presentation would be factual or dry and much less exciting to hear.

Exhorters are creative thinkers. They are known for their ideas. It you reject their first idea they will gladly give you another one. These are the eternal optimists whose glass is never half empty. They have foresight and are people of vision.

My friend Sally, an Exhorter, was experiencing a problem that seemed insurmountable. She described it as though she were standing at the base of a mountain, with the mountain looming in front of her. The mountain seemed so massive to her that she did not see how she would be able to climb over it or go around it. When Sally prayed about this situation, she gained a new perspective and was able to overcome the problem when God encouraged her to step back so that she could view the entire mountain. When she did this, the full mountain came into view and God gave her the ability to see Him leaning over it, arms outstretched, waiting to lift her up and carry her over the mountain,

It is easy to confuse the Exhorter's vision with that of the Prophet, but an Exhorter's vision is broad—he sees everything *across* the board, whereas the Prophet's vision is deep—he sees everything *through* the board.

Exhorters have a vision for affecting the masses. They are highly effective communicators with an ability to bridge the gap between social, economic, and religious diversity. These are the people whose names are recorded in the history books credited with changing the course of human events.

Exhorters are enthusiastic about causes. When they believe in something, they are able to motivate and inspire others to 'get on board'. We have all met them—they are the people that convince us to support a cause, purchase a product, or join a group. They spur us on, convincing us we that we should never give up on ourselves.

What would our lives be like without Exhorters? We would be limited from reaching our potential, left standing at the base of the mountain, because there would be no one to show us the way over it. Life would remain the status quo.

THE GIVER

Givers are designed to be the stewards of the world's resources. They can be described as Providers, Suppliers, Coordinators, Contributors, or Protectors. Givers recognize the value of material resources that are vital to human life and have a keen understanding of how to make the best use of them. They are proficient at preserving and protecting resources for future generations. Something a Giver might say is, "You paid too much for that."

We tend to think of the gift of giving in terms of money; however, Givers relate to a wide range of people, needs, and resources. Examples of the resources with which they identify are property, equipment, food, water, forests, and all other natural resources that sustain or contribute to our quality of life. When he attended the Life Purpose Workshop, Al, a Giver, had recently retired. In the color choice exercise—which color would you choose to best describe your work?—he chose brown because it was the color of waste. His reason for attending the workshop was that he wanted the second half of his life to be purposeful and rewarding, and he wanted to make a difference in the kingdom. He desired to discover biblical truths and identity his functional gift so that he would know, beyond a doubt, that He was serving God.

At the beginning of the workshop, Al told us he believed his work in the state's Water Resources Department had been secular work. After hearing God's truths about work, Al discovered he had been doing God's work all along, using his functional gift of Giver to develop a one-hundred-year water plan to preserve water for future generations.

God uses Givers to store up 'warehouses' of provision for others. People are naturally drawn to Givers when they have a material need because resources naturally flow into the Giver's arms.

What might life be like with no Givers? We would squander or use up all of the resources God has given us and there would be no more supply.

THE LEADER

Leaders empower others to accomplish goals. They are the 'vision-catchers' who grasp the ideas of others and are able to

119

bring them to reality. Leaders can be described as Administrators, Implementers, Managers, or Overseers. However, the functional gift of Leader is *not* a position; if you have this gift, becoming a manager or an administrator may not necessarily be right for you.

Leaders have a natural ability to nurture growth in our area of gifting. These are the people who grew the mom-and-pop businesses of yesteryear to the next level and the next, eventually propelling the enterprises to global proportions. Something a Leader might say is, "Do you have a plan?" Leaders are the ones who believe you don't have a plan if it is not in writing.

One of the Leader's greatest strengths is his ability to mobilize people with other gifts and empower them to do what they are designed to do. When Leaders grasp a vision, they are able to identify the right people with exactly the right gifts to bring that vision to reality.

After years of meeting with Christians and assessing their functional gifts, I am of the belief that there is not one Leader for every Prophet, Server, Teacher, Giver, and so on. God authored our work and He knew the precise number of gifts needed to 'care for the garden'. In His sovereignty, God distributed functional gifts on the basis of the work to be done as opposed to distributing them on an equal basis. Fewer Leaders are needed because God designed each of us to be leaders in our area of gifting.

When we are using our primary functional gift, doing the work God designed us to do, we are fully capable of working without constant direction or supervision. Consider Adam. God gave Adam his work assignments and Adam knew precisely what to do. God the Father, Leader of the Godhead, Overseer of all, checked in with Adam each day, but the Bible does not reveal a picture of God standing over Adam managing his every move. God gave Adam exactly the right gift for completing the garden work before him and then entrusted Adam to accomplish it.

The same holds true for the Leader. When God designed Leaders, He did not do so with the intention that they would stand over the Teachers, Givers, Servers, and other gifted people, telling them how to do their work. He designed the Leader's role to be similar to that of His role with Adam.

Leaders are designed to develop plans for accomplishing goals that bring the visions of others to reality. Developing plans and breaking them down into incremental steps come naturally to them. They are created with a capacity to bring people together and empower them to complete their work. Leaders are designed to provide opportunities for the rest of us to develop our God-given gifts by providing work assignments that fit with our gifting.

When problems arise, the Leader interacts with the workers to resolve the problem but he is not their watchdog. The Leader oversees the plan and keeps the project on track. If he sees the plan is not working, he changes it.

Imagine how different things would be if we were all doing the work God designed us to do, using our God-given gift. An effective Leader understands this concept and joyfully embraces the true biblical meaning of leadership.

During the twenty years I worked in the corporate world I met only one Leader and I was indeed fortunate to work for him. Hal prayerfully sought God's will for all of his employees and earnestly desired to empower them to reach their God-given potential.

I started working for Hal when God led the recruiter to call me when I was going to be fired from the school. Had I changed employment a year earlier during the time I had struck out on my own to find a job, I would not have worked for Hal. God had promoted him into his position of leadership at the electronics company during the time I worked at the school.

Working for Hal was one of the greatest joys of my work life. He prayed for me daily and handpicked my assignments to provide opportunity for me to use and develop my gift of Prophet. He challenged me to take on new assignments to stretch me and help me grow. Through Hal's guidance, I learned to embrace my gift of Prophet and celebrate the diversity of gifts God had given my coworkers and peers.

It is easy to confuse the functional gift of Leader with the functional gift of Server. Servers are extremely capable. They get the job done and, therefore, appear to have good leadership abilities. But Servers are designed to meet the physical needs of others. Leaders are designed by God to capture visions of others and bring them to reality. Leaders are designed to delegate; Servers are hands-on, designed to accomplish their assignments independently. The focus of the Leader is far-reaching whereas the focus of the Server is immediate. When a Server is asked to develop a ten-year plan, he is being asked to do something God never intended him to do. When a Server accepts a position of leadership, he may be setting himself up for failure.

If you have ever worked under someone with the functional gift of Leader, such as Hal, you will recognize him. When this occurs, you will find that the Leader is more interested in empowering you to do the work than standing over you and telling you how to do it.

What would life be like without them? If there were no Leaders, we would operate in chaos. There would be no written plans, no oversight, no business growth, and no opportunity for us to develop our gift and fulfill our God-given potential.

THE MERCIFUL

The Merciful is designed to bring hope and encouragement in the area of emotional needs. Their desire is to protect people from emotional hurt and bring healing. Mercifuls are particularly sensitive to those who are emotionally wounded or rejected. A person with this gift might say something like, "I feel your pain." And they do.

Mercifuls can be described as Compassionate, Tender-hearted, Sympathetic, or Kind. These are the relationship builders. For them, relationships take priority over everything else.

Mercifuls are good listeners. You may see them having coffee with a friend, listening intently, offering their comfort and personal support. They possess the unique ability to sense the moods or feelings of another person or group. They are slow to speak because they gauge their words carefully on the basis of how others may feel about what they will say.

We sometimes confuse the functional gift of Serving with the functional gift of Mercy because both are designed to meet needs. However, the Server is designed to meet the physical, practical needs of others whereas the Merciful is designed to contribute to the emotional needs of others. Mercifuls are attuned to matters of the heart while Servers are attuned to matters of the physical. They live by the motto "Home is where the heart is" whereas Servers live by the motto "Well done is always better than well said."

When I taught the Life Purpose Workshop, Butch and I often divided people into groups according to their functional gifts. Meeting with like-minded people provided comfort to the attendees as they were able to converse with people who shared their same perspective. Because they shared the same primary functional gift it was easy for them to identify with one another.

Butch and I frequently walked around to observe the interactions within the groups to make sure things were going well. As could be expected, the majority of the participants were enjoying the experience—talking, joking, and laughing. But one time, when we approached a group of Mercifuls, we saw that they were all crying—women and men alike. When we asked what had happened, they explained that they had been sharing deep, personal, heartfelt situations they had experienced throughout their lives. This touched them so deeply that it made them cry. Crying came naturally to them because God designed them to extend their emotional support. Mercifuls bring a heightened sensitivity to relationships those of us with other gifts are unable to convey.

When you think about the people in your life who have reached out to you in times of emotional pain and brokenness, they most likely have the functional gift of Mercy. These are the people you migrate to when you need someone to listen or you need a gentle touch or hug. They are emotionally safe to be around. When you are with them, you do not feel the need to hide your feelings or to 'put on a happy face'.

What would life be like without them? Were it not for the Merciful, we would live in a world void of love, empathy, compassion, kindness, and healthy relationships.

THE SEVEN FUNCTIONAL GIFTS IN ACTION

Understanding the characteristics of the seven functional gifts is key to embracing God's design for us. We have been created by God to contribute to the lives of others, and the best way to reach out to them is in ways that are consistent with our primary functional gift.

Let's evaluate the seven functional gifts in light of a person with a financial problem to see how each gift responds. We will see that all of the gifts are needed and of equal value; no gift is 'less than' or less needed than another.

The **Prophet** looks deep into the problem and realizes the person is violating basic financial principles. Even though the Prophet is not an expert in finance, he is able to identify relevant concepts that he can share with the person. He boldly states that the person will never be able to resolve his financial problems as long as he continues to violate these principles.

The **Server** offers practical support and assistance. He rolls up his shirtsleeves, sits down with the person, and balances his checkbook.

The **Teacher** opens his briefcase and removes financial management software, loads it onto the person's computer, and shows him how to use it. He evaluates all of the information and puts it on a spreadsheet so the person can track his expenses and spending. The Teacher may also give the person a book on financial planning or invite him to a financial seminar.

The **Exhorter** sees the problem from a broad perspective. He inspires the person to look beyond his immediate problem to see the possibilities for becoming financially independent. The Exhorter draws on personal experience to encourage and inspire the person and shares stories of other people who have achieved financial independence.

The **Giver** looks around the house, takes it all in and asks how much the person paid for everything. From his perspective, lack of income is not the issue; the real cause of the problem is how the money had been spent. The Giver will explain how resources should be used wisely.

The **Leader** wants to know what the person's financial vision is for the future. Once he understands this, he will develop an action plan and break it down into incremental steps so the person can follow it. Then he will look around at the other people in the room and, realizing the person is in good hands, he will excuse himself. He will assure the person that he will check back in periodically to see how the plan is working. The Leader will gladly change the plan if he sees it is not working.

The **Merciful** identifies with the person's feelings. He understands the person's pain and encourages him to talk about it. The Merciful puts his arm around the person, gives him a hug and assures him he is not alone.

Whichever gift we have, it is rewarding to be where God calls us to be, doing what He created us to do. It inspires and motivates us to discover our functional gift. (See Appendix A, page 151, for statements to help you begin to discern your primary functional gift or visit www.lifepurpose.com)

CHAPTER TEN

A Place for You

Discovering the Place God Has Prepared for You

*"...walk worthy of the vocation wherewith ye are called,
with all lowliness and meekness, with long suffering, forbearing
one another in love. ..."* —EPHESIANS 4:1b-2 (KJV)

I had the privilege of taking my grandson, Wyland, to
vacation bible school when he was little. Wyland was so excited
he could not stop talking about the fun he would have during the
week—that is, until we drove into the church parking lot.
Suddenly he was not so sure he wanted to attend. Wyland would
not leave my side when we arrived at his classroom. Never
having been to this church, he was unfamiliar with the
surroundings. Wyland was so frightened that he clung to me and
cried.

I gently guided him inside the door and toward the back of
the room where we were able to watch the other children when
they entered. Wiping Wyland's tears from his eyes and hugging
him tightly, I promised I would stay with him for as long as he
needed me.

Before long, Wyland peeked around me to watch the other
children putting their swim clothes into small baskets inside
some bookshelves. Then he started tugging at my skirt. Looking
up at me through teary eyes, he inquired if one of the baskets
was for him.

I walked Wyland over to the little baskets and pointed to the
one with his name on it. I pulled the basket from the shelf and

Wyland carefully laid his swimsuit and towel in it. He then grabbed my hand and returned to the safety of the back corner.

Wyland watched as the other children sat at the tables that had been prepared for them. Milk and cookies had been arranged next to each child's nametag.

Soon Wyland was yanking at my skirt again. He wanted to know if he had a place at one of the tables. Similar to Goldilocks in the story, *The Three Bears*, Wyland was looking for his 'place' or 'fit' in the room. He was ready for me to leave when he found his seat at one of the tables.

Discovering the place that had been prepared in advance for him gave Wyland a sense of security. Knowing that someone had prepared a place for him gave him confidence. Similar to Wyland, we are all looking for our place in life, the place where we feel we fit.

God has prepared a place for each of us that fits perfectly with His design for us. Like Adam in the garden, everything we will ever need is there. When we are in that place, we are free to be *who* God created us to be and do *what* He has designed us to do. We become like Wyland, confident and secure. When we are not in that place, we feel restless and unfulfilled. We lack passion. The sense of purpose for which we have been created eludes us.

Disneyland is called 'the happiest place on earth' because we do not have any cares when we are there. The Disney folks have anticipated our every need. When we enter the gate, we put ourselves into Disney's hands. We feel exhilarated and fearless, able to face whatever comes our way, even on the scariest of rides. This is also the way we feel when we are in the place God has prepared for us. If we were a paintbrush, we would feel as

128

though we were in paintbrush heaven. If we were a saw, we would feel as though we were in saw heaven.

Butch and I experienced these feelings when we went to Europe in 1996 to celebrate our ninth wedding anniversary. The first place I wanted to visit was Oxford, England. For me, this was my 'Disneyland' and I could think of no place on earth I would rather be. On arrival, I immediately grabbed a map and organized our day. Concerned about not having enough time to see all the sights, I attempted to squeeze as much into the day as possible. My plan was to grab a quick lunch along the way and eat it 'on the run' to avoid wasting time at a restaurant. Butch, however, had a different plan.

As I merrily raced through the streets pointing out the sights, I looked around to see if Butch shared my excitement. My first clue that he did not came when I saw him standing in front of a muffin shop looking over the menu, apparently not interested in a word I had been saying. I quickly ran back to where Butch was and grabbed his arm in an attempt to pull him along. My second clue came when he insisted we take a break, share a muffin and coffee, and just relax. "Relax?" I said in astonishment. How could we relax when there was so much to see?

The next leg of our journey took us to Germany. The first place Butch wanted to visit was an industrial museum. For Butch, that museum was his 'Disneyland'.

He immediately grabbed my arm and led me to the floor with the farm equipment. His plan was to spend the entire day in the museum and grab a quick lunch at the express counter to make the most of our time. He stressed the importance of staying with the plan so we could see everything.

Watching Butch excitedly racing through the exhibits was a new experience for me. Excitement was not something he showed very often and 'racing' was something I had never seen him do.

Despite Butch's enthusiasm, I soon became bored. Just how many tractors did we need to see? Before long, I spotted an eatery. Maybe a coffee and muffin would be a good way to relax. Butch interrupted my thoughts when he grabbed my arm and attempted to pull me along to see more exhibits. He was excited to show me the exact type of tractor he had learned to drive on the farm, but my interest had waned and I needed a break. I sat down at one of the tables and told Butch I wanted to relax. "Relax?" he said. How could we relax when there was so much to see?

In both of these situations, Butch and I were operating in environments that were in accordance with our primary functional gift. My ideal environment is knowledge-based. As a Prophet, I thrive on learning and gathering information and drawing on principles to solve problems. For me, standing in the middle of Oxford, England was like standing in the information capital of the world. It was the place where some of the greatest minds expanded their knowledge and drew on principles to solve some of the world's greatest problems. Visiting Oxford motivated me into action. It inspired me to race through the streets so as not to miss a single experience.

Butch is a Server. Servers are designed to meet the physical, practical needs of others. Their ideal environment is one where they can be hands-on, making use of equipment, tools, and other materials to accomplish or produce something.   For Butch, the tractors and farm equipment brought back memories of working on the farm, increasing productivity, and producing the best potato harvest his father had ever had. The farm equipment motivated Butch into action. It caused him to race from exhibit to exhibit, recalling the time on the farm when he did his best work, was a witness to his father, and experienced God working in and through him daily.

FINDING YOUR PLACE IN THE BODY

God loves us so much that He has prepared a place for each of us on earth. He is continuously working out His plans and purposes for us in this life and for eternity. But as Christians, we are also part of something far greater—the Body of Christ.

God's purpose for the Church extends well beyond that of one individual. He created us to work together in harmony. Our greatest opportunity as believers is to come together as a whole, devoting ourselves to the work God has put before us, embracing the uniqueness of our design, and celebrating the gift He has given us. Each functional gift is designed to contribute in a specific way, but we are most effective when all of the gifts are working together, as the following story illustrates.

Seven people, representing each of the functional gifts—Prophet, Server, Teacher, Exhorter, Leader, Giver, and Merciful—are walking down the street. They notice something in the back of an alleyway and decide to investigate. As they walk down the alley toward the object, the stench becomes overwhelming, but they continue walking toward it. They soon discover the 'object' is a human being, dressed in filthy rags, curled in a fetal position. He is so high on alcohol or drugs that he is unaware of their presence.

If Christ were there, He would pick up the addict and restore him to wholeness. He could do this because He has 100 % of all of the functional gifts, whereas none of us do. Jesus is with the Father in heaven, but His work on earth is not finished. The Holy Spirit empowers us to participate in Christ's work, to care for the 'garden' and to have an impact on the lives of others. We are Jesus' eyes, hands, feet, mind, mouth, arms, shoulders, and heart. As members of His Body, we share equally in restoring the addict. Our role in the Body was reserved in advance for us by God in accordance with our primary functional gift.

When I taught the Life Purpose Workshop, I used Don and Katie Fortune's *Motivational Gift Assessment* with permission. I have now developed my own assessment but their materials identified the relationship between each gift and the corresponding part of the Body that I have used in this book. The stories, examples, and descriptions associated with each gift come from my personal studies and experience.

The Prophet is the 'Eyes' of the body, its vision. God uses the Prophet to communicate principles of living to help the addict break free from his dependency and experience life to the fullest.

The Server is the 'Hands and Feet' of the Body. God uses the Server to meet the addict's immediate practical and physical needs. The Server will take the addict home, feed him, and give him a bath and a place to sleep for the night.

The Teacher is the 'Mind' of the Body. God uses him to feed the addict's intellect and nourish his soul in his recovery.

The Exhorter is the 'Mouth' of the Body. God uses the Exhorter to inspire the addict to move beyond his immediate situation—to enable him to see the possibilities for addiction free living.

The Giver is the 'Arms' of the Body. God uses him to bring the addict much needed provision—shelter, transportation, and opportunities for employment.

The Leader is the 'Shoulders' of the Body. God uses the Leader to develop a life plan for the addict and break it down into a series of steps that are easy to follow. The Leader also empowers people with other functional gifts to contribute to the addict's healing.

The Merciful is the 'Heart' of the Body. God uses the Merciful to confirm His love for the addict. The Merciful puts his arms around the addict, gives him support, and prays for him.

Exercising our primary functional gift is our full-time ministry. God sent His Son into the world and He is still sending Him through every believer. We are Christ's representatives on earth spiritually, relationally, and physically. True ministry occurs wherever God places us. It starts with our relationship with God and extends to the people He draws into our sphere of influence and authority.

A PICTURE OF CHRIST

The story of the addict shows us how God has uniquely designed us to work together to contribute to the lives of others. It demonstrates how cooking a meal, giving a person a bath, providing shelter, or something as simple as putting an arm around another person is kingdom work. That's how it was when Butch watered the dirt. He never said a word but he ministered to the two women through his actions. These stories help us to understand the impact we have when we operate within the framework of our primary functional gift.

When we use our functional gift the impact is greater than meets the eye. Many of us, when we were very young, completed a dot-to-dot picture in a coloring book. The picture began to evolve when we connected the dots. The real reward came when all of the dots were connected.

If life was a dot-to-dot drawing and we were creating a picture of Jesus Christ, all seven functional gifts would be required to complete the picture. Each individual gift would play a significant role in completing it and each would present an aspect of the nature and character of Christ. When all seven gifts work together the world sees a perfect picture of Christ.

The Prophet understands the underlying concepts used to create the picture. It is as though he is able to go underneath the picture to see how it was constructed, structurally. He is then able to share these concepts with others to help them make the connection between the dots.

Servers are 'dot-sitters'. They stand with us on the dots ready to meet our physical and practical needs to enable us to move from one dot to the next.

Teachers provide truth that nourishes our soul and lights the pathway between the dots so we can see where we are going.

Exhorters are able to overcome obstacles that prevent us from moving to the next dot. They see the possibilities for completing the picture and are able to inspire us to continue moving forward.

Givers provide the resources we need to journey from dot to dot, bringing a virtual backpack full of supplies.

Leaders keep their eyes on all of the dots to keep everyone on track.

Mercifuls reach out to us along the way, helping us to overcome the emotional scars and wounds that prevent us from moving to the next dot.

The illustration of the dot-to-dot picture reveals how each functional gift is designed to contribute to the lives of others and reveal the glory of God. When one believer is doing what God created him to do, operating by grace, Christ is revealed. When seven people work together by grace, each with a different functional gift, they present a mural of Christ to the broken world.

As believers, we need to ask ourselves what kind of picture we are presenting to the world. What does the world see through us as God's people? Are our actions and behavior consistent with the Word of God? Are we working within the area of our design, operating within our sphere of influence and authority, completing the work God has prepared for us? Are we operating by grace through faith? Or are we working through our own perceived strength?

I have thought a lot about these truths, particularly when Butch died. I also thought about them when Janne and I wrote this book after his death. When God led me to share our personal stories, I was uncertain whether to say Butch *was* or Butch *is*. But I know Butch is alive. He is living in a different realm but he is still very much the same.

Butch was a Server on earth and He is a Server in the eternal realm. He is using his functional gift in the heavenly realm to serve and glorify God. Butch never lost spiritual consciousness when he departed this earth and his emotions, intellect, personality, gifts, and memory went with him. Knowing Butch, when he met Noah he probably said, "Noah, let me talk to you about that ark."

I will see Butch again someday. In the new earth we will continue to be in full time ministry. If God is willing we may even be on the same ministry team.

The following excerpts are from *The Glories of Heaven*, an article written by Erwin W. Lutzer that appeared in the May/June 2001 edition of *Moody* magazine. A friend gave it to me after Butch's funeral service.

"What can you expect as a believer one minute after you die? While relatives sorrow on earth, you will find yourself in new surroundings, which just now are beyond our imagination. Most probably, you will see angels who have been assigned to escort you to your destination, just as the angels carried Lazarus to "Abraham's bosom" Luke 16.22 (NASB).

"You are keenly aware that you have arrived in heaven, and as you enter its gates, you see Christ who welcomes you home. Since He stood to welcome Stephen into the glories of heaven (Acts 7:56), it is reasonable to believe He will be on hand to bid you enter.

"You know who He is, and He quite obviously knows who you are. Because you are one of His sheep, He calls you by name. You look into His eyes and see compassion, love, and understanding. Though you feel altogether unworthy, you know His welcome is genuine. You see His nail prints, which trigger memories that make you fall on your face and worship. Were it not for His tender hand helping you to your feet, you would not be able to get up.

"So much is different, yet you are quite the same. You have entered heaven without a break in consciousness. Back on earth your friends will bury your body, but they cannot bury you. Just

before Stephen died, he said, 'Lord Jesus, receive my spirit"; he did not say, 'receive my body" (Acts 7:59)...

"One minute after we die our minds, our memories, will be clearer than ever before. We are reminded of Jesus' story in Luke 16 of the rich man who went to Hades with his memory intact. He knew his family on earth, pleading, 'I have five brothers' (v28). Death does not change what we know. Our personality will go on with the same information we have stored in our mind today.

"Think back to your background: your parents, brothers, sisters, family reunions. You will remember all of this and more in heaven. Do you actually suspect you might know less in heaven than you do on earth? Unthinkable!

"Once in heaven we will soon meet a host of others; some known to us in this life or through the pages of church history, others nameless in this world but equally honored in the world to come. On the Mount of Transfiguration, three of the disciples met Moses and Elijah (Matthew 17:1–8). So far as we know, there was no need for introductions; no need for nametags. In heaven there will be intuitive knowledge, for our minds will be redeemed from the limitations sin imposed on them.

"Think of your purest joy on earth; then multiply that many times, and you might catch a glimpse of heaven's euphoria...

"In heaven we will rest, but it is not the rest of inactivity. We will most probably continue many of the same kinds of activities we knew on earth. Artists will create art as never before; the scientist might be invited to continue his exploration of God's magnificent creation. The musicians will perform music; all of us will continue to learn.

"We can be sure that we will be the same people we were on earth; the same thoughts, feelings, and desires. Though our struggles with sin will be over, we will be aware of who we really are. There will be no doubt in our minds that we have just moved from one place to another.

"The real you will be there."...

In eternity we will be living and working in a Master-planned community built by the Master's hands. We will be doing what God created us to do, fulfilling our function of life. If He designed us to be a Prophet here, we will be a Prophet there. If He designed us to be a Server here, we will be a Server in the new earth. Our functional gift will not change. The depth and breadth of our assignments in the new earth will be determined by our faithfulness here. This life is a training ground for the life to come. The work God has prepared for us here is in preparation for our work assignments in the new earth. Those who are faithful to serve God in this life will be given greater responsibility in the new earth.

If we are to be successful in our endeavor to serve and glorify God and operate by grace, we need to step onto the bridge and begin to apply God's truths to our daily lives and work. There will be challenges along the way, but with God's help, we will be prepared to meet them.

For Prophets, the challenge is to go deep in relationship with God. Spend time with Him. Study His Word. As the 'Eyes' of the Body, when you spend time with God He will improve your vision.

The challenge for Servers, as the 'Feet and Hands' of the Body, is to be available to God first. Servers are so willing to serve others, it is easy for them to take on more than God intends. When they take on too much they become spread too thin and are less effective. They need to prayerfully consider each assignment before accepting it. To become most effective Servers need to learn to say, "No." Spend time with God daily, lifting your hands to God, asking Him how He wants to use them. Lift your feet to the Lord, asking Him where He wants you to walk. Then be still and wait for God to show you.

For Teachers, as the 'Mind' of the Body, the challenge is to study the Word and experience the presence of the Living God. God is truth and Teachers are designed to know and experience truth—to sense it, feel it, taste it, and enter into it. Spend time with God studying His Word. You have the capacity to enter into His presence and experience Him in ways that exceed the ability of the other gifts to do so.

The Exhorter's challenge is to gain God's perspective and make Him a priority over all other relationships. As the 'Mouth' of the Body, Exhorters are designed to inspire others to reach the potential God has placed in them. To become a source of encouragement to others, seek God's perspective in all things.

For Givers the challenge is to find security in God rather than the material resources of this world. God uses Givers as the 'Arms' to be vessels through which His resources flow. Trust God to work through you to store up 'warehouses' of supply for future generations instead of relying on your own self-sufficiency.

As the 'Shoulders' of the Body, Leaders have a dual challenge. The first is to submit to God, learning to rely on Him rather than yourself. The second challenge for Leaders is to learn to listen to God and respond in obedience. This is especially important because Leaders can easily overlook issues of integrity to achieve their objectives. In God's kingdom economy integrity is a must. God never uses His power and authority at the expense of His honor and integrity and neither should Leaders. Examine yourself on a daily basis to make sure you are walking in faith and relying exclusively on the power and authority of God.

The Mercifuls' challenge is to spend time with God to experience His love and compassion, to ask Him to reveal the areas where they have been wounded so He can bring wholeness. Mercifuls will then be drawn into deeper intimacy with God and others. If they do not do this, they will operate out of their own woundedness instead of God's love and make decisions on the basis of feelings instead of God's truths. This runs the risk of not only damaging themselves but also the people around them. As the 'Heart' of the Body, spend time with God so He can heal the areas where your heart has been wounded. This will empower you to reach out to others to reveal God's love to a broken world.

PERSONAL CHALLENGE

God wants to bring you into your sphere of influence and authority and teach you to walk in His ways. This will not happen overnight. Learning to apply God's truths and operate by grace is a process. There will be times when you feel as though you have both feet in the heavenly realm. There will also be times when you feel as though you are in the desert, wondering where you made a wrong turn. If you are faithful to use the gift God gave you, you will be confident and secure and the world will begin to see a very different picture of Jesus Christ through you.

CHAPTER ELEVEN

Hearing the Knock
The Still, Small Voice of God

"Ask, and it will be given to you; seek, and you will find; knock, and it will be opened to you."
—MATTHEW 7:7 (NAS)

Paul makes numerous references in the New Testament to running a race:

"Do you not know that in a race all the runners run, but only one gets the prize? Run in such a way as to get the prize."
— I CORINTHIANS 9:24

He instructs us to press on toward the goal to which we are called:

"...I press on toward the goal to win the prize for which God has called me heavenward in Christ Jesus."
—PHILIPPIANS 3:14

Crossing the bridge, keeping our eyes fixed on God and completing the work He has prepared for us is part of our race. God has laid out a course for each of us according to His plans and purposes for our lives and He designed us to run effectively. Running requires perseverance and trust in Him. To successfully keep our eyes fixed on God, we need to dialogue with Him in prayer and study His Word. We will experience hurdles along the way, even when we are operating within our sphere of influence and authority. There will be times when we will feel disillusioned and want to quit. But for a believer, quitting should never be an option.

God created us to serve and glorify Him. He longs to use us in His service and delight ourselves in Him. When we are involved in kingdom work, we experience the sense of purpose and significance for which we were created.

After reading this book you may desire to approach work differently. You may yearn to experience the joy of serving and glorifying God daily but you are filled with uncertainty, questioning if you are on the right track. You may feel like a plow horse running on the Indy 500 race track, ill-suited for your present line of work. You may sense that you need to change direction but you don't know how to alter your course. If this describes your situation, it is important to realize you did not arrive here overnight. You stepped outside of God's grace into the world economy one ring at a time and it will take time for God to reposition you. If you stand firm and keep your eyes fixed on Him, He will be faithful to redirect your steps.

Perhaps you are functioning within your sphere of influence and authority, operating by faith, experiencing God's grace. You sense God is expanding your sphere of influence and authority, saying, "Well done." I encourage you to stand firm and do not run ahead of Him. Wait for God to reveal your next assignment.

If you are unemployed you may be experiencing a great deal of stress. You are trying to pursue God's direction but well-meaning family members or friends may constantly be pushing you to do something, anything—just get a job! If your unemployment persists, they may conclude you are not trying hard enough or you are unwilling to work.

Regardless of your situation, trust God to reveal *His* work for you. He knows the path on which He wants to establish you and He will direct your steps. God wants you to experience biblical success: *bringing glory to God on earth by completing the work He gives us to do.* When you wait on God, trusting Him with your future, He will accomplish all that He has prepared for you. He will bring you to the finish line where you will join the great cloud of witnesses who crossed before you:

"Therefore, since we are surrounded by such a great cloud of witnesses, let us throw off everything that hinders and the sin that so easily entangle. And let us run with perseverance the race marked out for us..." —HEBREWS 12:1

Today is a new day in your relationship with God. Whether you are in the middle of the good times, difficult times, or the wait times:

- Keep your eyes fixed on God, trusting Him in all situations.

- Talk with God in prayer. Ask Him to reveal His plans and purposes for your daily life and work. Tell Him you want your work to become your full-time ministry and your spiritual act of worship. Ask God to help you run your race with perseverance.

- Study the Bible. Read the account of Joseph in the Old Testament to observe how God worked in his life to fulfill His plans and purposes for him and prepare him for greater responsibility.

- Rest in the truth that God is your Provider. Look for ways in which He is making His provision known to you. Thank Him for everything He has given you.

The greatest challenge before each of us, if we are to run the race to win the prize, is to learn to listen to God. Many have listened to the world so long and so intently that they are no longer attuned to God's voice. They do not hear 'the knock'.

There is a story about a Native American and his friend walking through the streets of Chicago. The two are bombarded by the din of the crowds yet the Native American tells his friend that he hears a cricket. His friend, in disbelief, challenges the truth of this statement. The Native American, beckoning his friend to follow him, walks to a bush and lifts a leaf to reveal the cricket. Astonished, the friend questions him as to how he could hear such a tiny sound above the overpowering noise. The Native American responds, "It depends on what you listen to." He then drops a handful of coins on the sidewalk. People everywhere stopped and looked toward the sound.

We hear that to which we want to listen. As Christians, when we choose to live and work in the secular world economy, we can become so immersed in the activities around us that we fail to listen. If we choose to make our way across the bridge toward God's kingdom economy by grace through faith, we will learn to hear the tiniest of sounds, even the still small voice of God.

EPILOGUE

"Let us hear the conclusion of the whole matter:
Fear God and keep His commandments,
For this is man's all."
—ECCLESIASTES 12: 13 (NKJV)

Losing Butch was the most difficult season of my life. I still remember sitting in my living room chair, overcome with immense grief. I felt as though half of me had been cut away; life without Butch was more than I felt I could bear.

The anguish of Butch's death is a loss from which I have never fully recovered but slowly over time, I began to hear the still small voice of God. Drawing on the same truths that I presented in the Life Purpose Workshop, and now in this book, God gently reminded me that He had a plan and purpose for my life. Butch's earthly work was finished but God had more for me to do.

Eventually I began to heal and have hope for my future. This did not happen overnight. The healing was gradual—it occurred over time and it continues today. But it took eight years for me to learn to start over.

Writing this book has been the second most difficult season of my life. I reluctantly began writing in 2005, three years after Butch's death. This has also been an eight-year journey. The first five years were spent writing primarily because those who attended the Life Purpose Workshop and those who heard me on Moody Broadcasting's Midday Connection broadcasts told me this material needed to be available in book form. Yet those first five years were not wasted. God used them to bring additional healing and to shape me into the person I am today. He also used those years to deepen my level of understanding of His truths and develop my writing skills.

The final three years of writing this book were truly an act of grace and faith. I took that first step of faith in December 2010 when the Holy Spirit prompted me to cancel my holiday plans. I had arranged to spend the holidays in San Diego with a friend. The months leading up to Christmas were spent talking to my friend on the telephone making plans and discussing all the things we were going to do. Two weeks before I was to leave the Holy Spirit prompted me to stay home. Certain that I had heard Him incorrectly, I kept praying about the trip. I could not imagine why God would want me to spend Christmas at home, alone.

My requests to God for an explanation went unanswered. But the more I prayed, the more convinced I became that staying home was the right thing to do. Unable to deny the Holy Spirit's prompting, I called my friend to let her know I would not be coming. I had no idea what God had in store for me but San Diego was not a part of it.

Shortly after I canceled my trip another friend called. She wanted to spend Christmas Day together. Without giving it a second thought, I invited her to come to my house to watch Christmas movies and share dinner. Surely God would not mind if I spent the day with a friend. After all, I had obediently canceled my trip and I was staying home for the holidays. What would be wrong with spending Christmas Day with a friend?

It became apparent God truly wanted me to stay home alone when my friend called Christmas Eve to cancel our plans. She was sorry but she would not be coming over.

Uncertain of what to do on Christmas Day, I decided to work on this book. I spent the entire day writing, prayerfully asking God for clarity regarding how I could best serve Him. Late in the afternoon I was standing at the sink washing dishes, thinking about the book, when I heard the Holy Spirit say in my innermost being, "This is why you stayed home. I want you to write." I will never forget that moment for it was then that God released me to write this book. This was reconfirmed when Janne called me a few days later to tell me we had received an invitation from a publisher to submit our manuscript. In heeding God's directive to stay home, the time I spent writing on Christmas Day made it possible to send the first three chapters within one week.

The next three years were spent prayerfully writing and rewriting, studying, submitting and resubmitting the manuscript, receiving rejections, naming and renaming the book, and learning the 'ins and outs' of publishing. Sometimes that is the way it is when God directs us to do something—it is not always easy but He is faithful to accomplish what He sets out to do.

As Janne and I prepare for publishing this book, we have no idea of the outcome. But God does. He knows precisely what He wants to do with this book and we trust Him with the result.

Though I do not know what God has in store for my future, my life and work are in His hands. My prayer and heart's desire is to help God's people reach their potential in Christ—to help them step onto the bridge and experience all that God has prepared for them.

May God bless you and may you experience the richness of His grace.

Joanne Hawes

Statements to Help You Identify Your Primary Functional Gift

Carefully read each of the statements below to determine the **ONE** with which you **MOST** identify.

1. I can really relate to the statement, "Well done is always better than well said." (Server)
2. From my perspective, most problems could be solved if people would just make an effort to get along. (Merciful)
3. I believe there is no excuse for a lack of personal growth. (Exhorter)
4. Other people think of me as a 'penny pincher'. (Giver)
5. I loathe it when people are deceitful. (Prophet)
6. I am very comfortable stepping in and providing leadership when needed. (Leader)
7. I like nothing better than to spend hours studying. (Teacher)

Disclaimer: These statements are offered as a way to begin to identity your primary functional gift. They are neither scientific nor all-conclusive. They are intended to be used in conjunction with the truths presented in this book, combined with prayer and the study of God's Word. Ask the Spirit to confirm your gift and direct your steps. **For more information on functional gifts, please visit WWW.LIFEPURPOSE.COM**

Key Words and Phrases
Shown Alphabetically

BIBLICAL OBEDIENCE

The biblical definition of the word *obedience* contains a sense of immediacy. It can be described through the example of a knock at the door. When we hear a knock, we stop what we are doing and simply respond by answering the door.

BIBLICAL SUCCESS

Bringing glory to God on earth by completing the work He gave you to do.

BIBLICAL FAITH

Biblical faith waits on God with full assurance, trusting Him to meet all of our needs. It looks upward to God the Father and Jesus Christ the Son and inward to the Holy Spirit who indwells us. Biblical faith has full confidence that God can accomplish all of the work He has prepared in advance for us.

CONGRUENT

To be in complete agreement or harmony, physically, relationally, and spiritually.

FUNCTIONAL GIFTS

Functional gifts describe the function for which we have been created. They motivate us to action, providing the framework for the way we think, feel, make decisions, and relate to others. They are foundational to discovering God's purpose for our daily lives and work. Functional gifts may also be referred to as Motive

Gifts or Redemptive Gifts. Functional gifts are listed in Romans 12:6-8 (NAS).

GRACE

The empowering presence of the Holy Spirit enabling us to be *who* God has created us to be and do *what* He has designed us to do.

GRACE-BASED WORK

All work that is accomplished through the empowering presence of the Holy Spirit, regardless of where it takes place.

KINGDOM ECONOMY

The eternal system of righteousness governed by God.

LAW OF FAITH

The governing principle under which we live and work in God's kingdom economy.

LAW OF SIN AND DEATH

The governing principle under which we live and work in the world economy.

OFFICE GIFTS

Office gifts enable believers to function within a specific office of leadership in the corporate Body (the Church) for the purpose of directing the members. Not everyone has an office gift. Office gifts are listed in Ephesians 4:11-12 (NAS) and they do not change.

PHYSICAL ASPECT OF OUR BEING

The physical aspect of our being describes how God uniquely designed us to relate to and interact with physical world in which we live and work. (The Bible refers to this as our 'Body')

RELATIONAL ASPECT OF OUR BEING

The relational aspect of our being describes how God uniquely designed us to relate to other people. (The Bible refers to this as our 'Soul')

SECULAR

Without God.

SECULAR ECONOMY

The world system governed by mankind, apart from God.

SECULAR WORK

All work—religious or nonreligious—accomplished through the flesh, apart from grace.

SPHERE OF INFLUENCE AND AUTHORITY

The place God has prepared for each of us that is consistent with His plans and purposes for our lives and work. The work God prepared in advance for us lies within this sphere. When we are functioning by grace through faith in our sphere of influence and authority, the Holy Spirit draws people to us that have need of our gift.

SPIRITUAL ASPECT OF OUR BEING

The spiritual aspect of our being defines how God designed us to interact with and relate to Him. (The Bible refers to this as our 'Spirit')

SPIRITUAL GIFTS

Spiritual gifts are the manifestation or supernatural demonstration of the Holy Spirit working in a believer for the common good of the Body. They are not permanent. They come and go at the discretion of the Holy Spirit, operating at different times through different believers as God wills, to glorify Him and encourage the Body. Spiritual gifts are listed in I Corinthians 12:1, 7–11 (NAS)

TRINITY

The triune Godhead—Father, Son and Holy Spirit.

Key Bible Verses

Shown in the order presented in the book

"Trust in the Lord with all your heart and do not lean on your own understanding. In all your ways acknowledge Him, and He will make your paths straight."—PROVERBS 3:5, 6 (NAS)

"For we are His workmanship, created in Christ Jesus for good works, which God prepared beforehand so that we would walk in them." —EPHESIANS 2:10 (NAS)

"I have brought you glory on earth by finishing the work you gave me to do." —JOHN 17:4

"For You formed my inward parts; You wove me in my mother's womb." —PSALM 139:13 (NAS)

"For we are God's handiwork, created in Christ Jesus to do good works, which God prepared in advance for us to do."
—EPHESIANS 2:10

"To You I lift up my eyes, O You who are enthroned in the heavens!" —PSALM 123:1 (NAS)

"God is a righteous judge..." —PSALM 7:11a

"You are my King and my God, who decrees victories for Jacob." —PSALM 44:4

"Your throne, O God, will last for ever and ever; ..."
—PSALM 45:6

"Through him all things were made; without him nothing was made that has been made." —JOHN 1:3

"In My Father's house are many mansions; if it were not so, I would have told you. I go to prepare a place for you."
—JOHN 14:2 (NKJV)

"Then the LORD God formed a man from the dust of the ground and breathed into his nostrils the breath of life, and the man became a living being." —GENESIS 2:7

"And with that he breathed on them and said, 'Receive the Holy Spirit.'" —JOHN 20:22

"But the Helper, the Holy Spirit, whom the Father will send in My name, He will teach you all things, and bring to your remembrance all that I said to you." —JOHN 14:26 (NAS)

"But I tell you the truth, it is to your advantage that I go away; for if I do not go away, the Helper will not come to you; but if I go, I will send Him to you." —JOHN 16:7 (NAS)

"Then he continued, 'Do not be afraid, Daniel. Since the first day that you set your mind to gain understanding and to humble yourself before your God, your words were heard, and I have come in response to them. But the prince of the Persian kingdom resisted me twenty-one days. Then Michael, one of the chief princes, came to help me, because I was detained there with the king of Persia.'" —DANIEL 10:12-13

"Bless the Lord, you mighty angels of his who carry out his orders, listening for each of his commands. Yes, bless the Lord, you armies of his angels who serve Him constantly."
—PSALM 103:20-21 (TLB)

"Now the LORD God had planted a garden in the east, in Eden; and there he put the man he had formed." —GENESIS 2:8

"...rule over the fish of the sea and over the birds of the sky and over every living thing that moves on the earth."
—GENESIS 1:28b (NAS)

"When I consider your heavens, the work of your fingers, the moon and the stars, which you have set in place, what is mankind that you are mindful of them, human beings that you care for them? You have made them a little lower than the angels and crowned them with glory and honor. You made them rulers over the works of your hands; you put everything under their feet: all flocks and herds, and the animals of the wild, the birds in the sky, and the fish in the sea, all that swim the paths of the seas." —PSALM 8:3–8

"Therefore, just as through one man sin entered into the world, and death through sin, and so death spread to all men, because all sinned—" —ROMANS 5:12 (NAS)

"The man said, 'The woman you put here with me—she gave me some fruit from the tree, and I ate it.' Then the LORD God said to the woman, 'What is this you have done?' The woman said, 'The serpent deceived me, and I ate.' So the LORD God said to the serpent, 'Because you have done this, cursed are you above all livestock and all wild animals! ... To Adam he said, 'Because you listened to your wife and ate fruit from the tree about which I commanded you, "You must not eat from it," Cursed is the ground because of you; through painful toil you will eat food from it all the days of your life. It will produce thorns and thistles for you, and you will eat the plants of the field. By the sweat of your brow you will eat your food until you return to the ground, since from it you were taken; for dust you are and to dust you will return.'" —GENESIS 3:12–14a; 17–19

"...Cursed is the ground because of you; through painful toil you will eat food from it all the days of your life. It will produce thorns and thistles for you, and you will eat the plants of the field. By the sweat of your brow you will eat your food until you return to the ground, since from it you were taken; for dust you are and to dust you will return." —GENESIS 3:17-19

"More than that, I count all things to be loss in view of the surpassing value of knowing Christ Jesus my Lord, for whom I have suffered the loss of all things, and count them but rubbish so that I may gain Christ..." —PHILIPPIANS 3:8 (NAS)

158

"THE SPIRIT OF THE LORD IS UPON ME, BECAUSE HE ANOINTED ME TO PREACH THE GOSPEL TO THE POOR. HE HAS SENT ME TO PROCLAIM RELEASE TO THE CAPTIVES, AND RECOVERY OF SIGHT TO THE BLIND, TO SET FREE THOSE WHO ARE OPPRESSED, ... "

—LUKE 4:18 (NAS)

"And you were dead in your trespasses and sins, in which you formerly walked according to the course of this world, according to the prince of the power of the air, of the spirit that is now working in the sons of disobedience. Among them we too all formerly lived in the lusts of our flesh, indulging the desires of the flesh and of the mind, and were by nature children of wrath, even as the rest. But God, being rich in mercy, because of His great love with which He loved us, even when we were dead in our transgressions, made us alive together with Christ (by grace you have been saved), and raised us up with Him, and seated us with Him in the heavenly places in Christ Jesus, ... "

—EPHESIANS 2:1–6 (NAS)

"...In this world you will have trouble. But take heart! I have overcome the world." —JOHN 16:33

"... I have learned to be content in whatever circumstances I am." —PHILIPPIANS 4:11 (NAS)

"But by the grace of God I am what I am, and his grace to me was not without effect. No, I worked harder than all of them—yet not I, but the grace of God that was with me."

—I CORINTHIANS 15:10

"So Paul and Barnabas spent considerable time there, speaking boldly for the Lord, who confirmed the message of his grace by enabling them to perform signs and wonders."

—ACTS 14:3

"You who are trying to be justified by law have been alienated from Christ; you have fallen away from grace."

—GALATIANS 5:4

"...Grace be with you." —Colossians 4:18

"The Word became flesh and made his dwelling among us. We have seen his glory, the glory of the one and only Son, who came from the Father, full of grace and truth. —JOHN 1:14

"Jesus answered, 'I am the way and the truth and the life. No one comes to the Father except through me.'" —JOHN 14:6

"But he said to me, 'My grace is sufficient for you, for my power is made perfect in weakness.'" — II CORINTHIANS 12:9a

"...I urge you to live a life worthy of the calling you have received... But to each one of us grace has been given as Christ apportioned it." —EPHESIANS 4:1,7 (NAS)

"And my God will meet all your needs according to the riches of his glory in Christ Jesus." —PHILIPPIANS 4:19

"But if serving the LORD seems undesirable to you, then choose for yourselves this day whom you will serve, whether the gods your ancestors served beyond the Euphrates, or the gods of the Amorites, in whose land you are living. But as for me and my household, we will serve the LORD." —JOSHUA 24:15

"...fixing our eyes on Jesus, the pioneer and perfecter of faith."
—HEBREWS 12:2b

"Therefore, since we have been justified through faith, we have peace with God through our Lord Jesus Christ, through whom we have gained access by faith into this grace in which we now stand..." —ROMANS 5:1–2

"For through the grace given to me I say to everyone among you not to think more highly of himself than he ought to think, but to think so as to have sound judgment, as God has allotted to each a measure of faith." —ROMANS 12:3 (NAS)

"Men have not heard nor perceived by the ear, nor has the eye seen any God besides You, Who acts for the one who waits for Him." —ISAIAH 64:4 (NKJV)

"...Truly I tell you, if you have faith as small as a mustard seed, you can say to this mountain, 'Move from here to there,' and it will move. Nothing will be impossible for you."
—MATTHEW 17:20b

"But he said to me, 'My grace is sufficient for you, for my power is made perfect in weakness.' Therefore I will boast all the more gladly about my weaknesses, so that Christ's power may rest on me." —II CORINTHIANS 12:9

"Whoever digs a hole and scoops it out falls into the pit they have made." —PSALM 7:15

"...You were faithful with a few things, I will put you in charge of many things..." —MATTHEW 25:21b (NAS)

"Whoever can be trusted with very little can also be trusted with much..." —LUKE 16:10a

"You intended to harm me, but God intended it for good to accomplish what is now being done, the saving of many lives."
—GENESIS 50:20

"Brethren, I do not regard myself as having laid hold of it yet; but one thing I do: forgetting what lies behind and reaching forward to what lies ahead, I press on toward the goal for the prize of the upward call of God in Christ Jesus."
—PHILIPPIANS 3:13–14 (NAS)

"For to me, to live is Christ and to die is gain."
—PHILIPPIANS 1:21

"For behold, I create new heavens and a new earth,..."
—ISAIAH 65:17a (NKJV)

" 'For as the new heavens and the new earth which I will make, shall remain before Me,' says the LORD, 'so shall your descendants and your name remain.' " — ISAIAH 66:22 (NKJV)

"Nevertheless we, according to His promise, look for new heavens and a new earth in which righteousness dwells."
—II PETER 3:13 (NKJV)

"Now I saw a new heaven and a new earth, for the first heaven and the first earth had passed away. Also there was no more sea. Then I, John, saw the holy city, New Jerusalem, coming down out of heaven from God, prepared as a bride adorned for her husband." —REVELATION 21:1–2 (NKJV)

"Then the angel showed me the river of the water of life, as clear as crystal, flowing from the throne of God and of the Lamb down the middle of the great street of the city. On each side of the river stood the tree of life, bearing twelve crops of fruit, yielding its fruit every month. And the leaves of the tree are for the healing of the nations. No longer will there be any curse. The throne of God and of the Lamb will be in the city, and his servants will serve him. They will see his face, and his name will be on their foreheads. There will be no more night. They will not need the light of a lamp or the light of the sun, for the Lord God will give them light. And they will reign forever and ever."
—REVELATION 22:1–5

"And I heard a loud voice from heaven saying, 'Behold, the tabernacle of God is with men, and He will dwell with them, and they shall be His people. God Himself will be with them and be their God'... 'These words are true and faithful'"

—REVELATION 21:3; 5 (NKJV)

"What use is it, my brethren, if someone says he has faith but he has no works? Can that faith save him?... Even so faith, if it has no works, is dead, being by itself. But someone may well say, 'You have faith and I have works; show me your faith without the works, and I will show you my faith by my works.'... But are you willing to recognize, you foolish fellow, that faith without works is useless? Was not Abraham our father justified by works when he offered up Isaac his son on the altar? You see that faith was working with his works, and as a result of the works, faith was perfected. ... You see that a man is justified by works and not by faith alone. ... For just as the body without the spirit is dead, so also faith without works is dead."

—JAMES 2:14, 17–18, 20–23, 26 (NAS)

"Then I heard a voice from heaven saying to me, 'Write: Blessed are the dead who die in the Lord from now on.'" "'Yes,' says the Spirit, 'that they may rest from their labors, and their works follow them.'" —REVELATION 14:13 (NKJV)

"I know that everything God does will remain forever..."

—ECCLESIASTES 3:14a (NAS)

"For God will bring every work into judgment, including every secret thing, Whether good or evil."

—ECCLESIASTES 12:14 (NKJV)

"And if you call on the Father, who without partiality judges according to each one's work, conduct yourselves throughout the time of your stay here in fear..." — I PETER 1:17 (NKJV)

"Also to You, O Lord, belongs mercy; for You render to each one according to his work." —PSALM 62:12 (NKJV)

"For we are God's fellow workers; you are God's field, you are God's building. According to the grace of God which was given to me, as a wise master builder I have laid the foundation, and another builds on it. But let each one take heed how he builds on it. For no other foundation can anyone lay than that which is laid, which is Jesus Christ. Now if anyone builds on this foundation with gold, silver, precious stones, wood, hay, straw, each one's work will become clear; for the Day will declare it, because it will be revealed by fire; and the fire will test each one's work, of what sort it is. If anyone's work which he has built on it endures, he will receive a reward. If anyone's work is burned, he will suffer loss; but he himself will be saved, yet so as through fire." —I CORINTHIANS 3:9–15 (NKJV)

"...rule over the fish of the sea and over the birds of the sky and over every living thing that moves on the earth."

—GENESIS 1:28b (NAS)

165

"Examine yourselves as to whether you are in the faith. Test yourselves. Do you not know yourselves, that Jesus Christ is in you?" —II CORINTHIANS 13:5 (NKJV)

"But by the grace of God I am what I am, and His grace toward me was not in vain; but I labored more abundantly than they all, yet not I, but the grace of God which was with me."
—I CORINTHIANS 15:10 (NKJV)

"...but through love serve one another."
—GALATIANS 5:13c (NAS)

"And He gave some as apostles, and some as prophets, and some as evangelists, and some as pastors and teachers, for the equipping of the saints for the work of service, to the building up of the body of Christ..." —EPHESIANS 4:11-12 (NAS)

"When the day of Pentecost had come, they were all together in one place. And suddenly there came from heaven a noise like a violent rushing wind, and it filled the whole house where they were sitting. And there appeared to them tongues as of fire distributing themselves, and they rested on each one of them. And they were all filled with the Holy Spirit and began to speak with other tongues, as the Spirit was giving them utterance." —ACTS 2:1-4 (NAS)

"Now concerning spiritual gifts, brethren, I do not want you to be unaware...But to each one is given the manifestation of the Spirit for the common good. For to one is given the word of wisdom through the Spirit, and to another the word of knowledge according to the same Spirit; to another faith by the same Spirit, and to another gifts of healing by the one Spirit, and to another the effecting of miracles, and to another prophecy, and to another the distinguishing of spirits, to another various kinds of tongues, and to another the interpretation of tongues. But one and the same Spirit works all these things, distributing to each one individually just as He wills" —I CORINTHIANS 12:1, 7–11 (NAS)

"Since we have gifts that differ according to the grace given to us, each of us is to exercise them accordingly: if prophecy, according to the proportion of his faith; if service, in his serving; or he who teaches, in his teaching; or he who exhorts, in his exhortation; he who gives, with liberality; he who leads, with diligence; he who shows mercy, with cheerfulness." —ROMANS 12:6–8 (NAS)

"...walk worthy of the vocation wherewith ye are called, with all lowliness and meekness, with long suffering, forbearing one another in love. ..." —EPHESIANS 4:1b,2 (KJV)

"Ask, and it will be given to you; seek, and you will find; knock, and it will be opened to you." —MATTHEW 7:7 (NAS)

"Do you not know that in a race all the runners run, but only one gets the prize? Run in such a way as to get the prize."
— I CORINTHIANS 9:24

"I press on toward the goal to win the prize for which God has called me heavenward in Christ Jesus."

—PHILIPPIANS 3:14

"Therefore, since we are surrounded by such a great cloud of witnesses, let us throw off everything that hinders and the sin that so easily entangles. And let us run with perseverance the race marked out for us…" —HEBREWS 12:1

""Let us hear the conclusion of the whole matter: Fear God and keep His commandments, For this is man's all."

—ECCLESIASTES 12: 13 (NKJV)

www.ingramcontent.com/pod-product-compliance
Lightning Source LLC
Chambersburg PA
CBHW072141090426
42739CB00013B/3244